TECHNOCRACY IN AMERICA

RISE OF THE INFO-STATE

PARAG KHANNA

ENDORSEMENTS

"American democracy is broken. But the best political practices of other countries can fix it. Read this book to find out how!"
 - Daniel Bell, author of *The China Model* and Dean, Faculty of Politics and Public Administration, Shandong University

What can America learn from the more technocratic governments in today's world? I don't agree with everything in this book, but it is one of the most important and urgent rethinkings of what has gone wrong in the United States."
 - Tyler Cowen, Professor of Economics, George Mason University, and author, *Average is Over*

"Parag Khanna does it again, brilliantly pushing the boundaries of how we must rethink technocracy and democracy in our densely connected, rapidly changing and radically contingent world. And in such a world we will need a new generation of technocrats who are well versed in complexity science and deep listening skills. This book should be read by all of us especially in light of our recent experiences picking our next president."
 - John Seely Brown, Former Chief Scientist, Xerox Corporation and Director of Xerox Palo Alto Research Center (PARC)

"Parag has produced yet another thoughtful and provocative masterpiece. His insights on technocracy, which focuses on performance rather than politics, stems from an astute and up-close observation of the Singaporean and Swiss systems, and he is among the very few who has this unique vantage point. I would highly recommend this book to anyone who wants to understand how to run a high-performing country or organisation. It will be one of the best investments you'll ever make."
 - Tan Yinglan, Venture Partner, Sequoia Capital, and author, The Way of the VC

Copyright © 2017 by Parag Khanna

All rights reserved.

www.paragkhanna.com

First Edition

ISBN: 978-0-9982325-1-5

Printed by CreateSpace

Print formatting and cover by Distillate

Images on cover used under license "Shutterstock.com"

CONTENTS

PROLOGUE: THE DIAGNOSIS — 1

1. EVOLUTION OF AN ARCHETYPE — 7
- The Secret to Success — 7
- A New State for a New Era — 11
- Beyond Democracy to Good Governance — 15

2. HOW TO RUN A COUNTRY — 23
- Switzerland: Too Small to Fail — 23
- Singapore: From Consent to Consultation — 26
- Securing the Info-State – and Citizens From It — 36
- Info-State as Innovation State — 40
- Warring for Talent — 44
- Small States, Big Ideas — 46

3. SEVEN PRESIDENTS ARE BETTER THAN ONE — 53
- From Oval Office to Round Table — 53
- The Best and the Brightest — 62
- The Meritocracy Behind Technocracy — 68
- The Technocratic Mantra: Utilitarianism — 72

4. PARLIAMENTS FOR THE PEOPLE — 75
- Politics Without Policy — 75
- Constant Contact: Democracy as Data — 80
- From Parties to Coalitions — 88
- Governors over Senators — 92
- The Rules of Law — 93

5. CALL IN THE TECHNOCRATS 99
    Getting Our House in Order 99
    The United Info-States of America 107
    Maintaining Global Influence 114

CONCLUSION: THE BEND OF HISTORY 119

ACKNOWLEDGMENTS 121
ABOUT THE AUTHOR 123

PROLOGUE: THE DIAGNOSIS

America's 2016 presidential election exposed that its style of democracy is as much a tool of division as unity. Two years of toxic campaigning revealed deep rifts in the nation's fabric while providing no common agenda for how to overcome them. Nearly two centuries after Alexis de Tocqueville's ode *Democracy in America*, it's time to admit that America needs less of its own version of democracy—much less.

Over the past decade, Americans have become accustomed to hearing that their position in the global rankings of wealth, life expectancy, education, public safety and other metrics has slid below that of their first world peers. If this wake-up call were not enough, a 2014 Gallup survey found that Americans are not only fed up with the performance of the federal government, but also that they have lost faith in their *system* of government, with dissatisfaction doubling to 65 percent. The flaw is both in delivery and design. Democracy alone just isn't good enough anymore.

America today far better represents degenerative politics than good governance. Many American intellectuals celebrate the theater of politics as if it is the embodiment of Tocqueville's praise for civic democracy. But democracy is not an end in itself. The greater goal is effective governance and improved national well-being. Because Americans no longer sense collective progress, they don't trust their institutions anymore, whether the White House, Congress, political parties, the Supreme Court, big business, or church. These organs of American leadership are passing down to the next generation a less well functioning government and society rather than the one they need to manage a complex future.

In his recent book *Political Order and Political Decay*, scholar Francis Fukuyama wonders whether the American system requires some kind of external "shock to the political order"—such as a war or revolution—to jolt itself out of the present downward spiral and return to a focus on performance rather than politics. Perhaps Donald Trump represented just such a shock. By taking the White House, while Republicans retained the Senate and House, Trump's populist revolution led many to fear that he represents a kind of tyranny that no checks and balances can prevent.

Democracy producing tyranny: Plato saw it coming. The ancient Greek philosopher articulated a range of possible regimes from aristocracy to tyranny, with democracy being the penultimate phase of degeneration. For Plato, the essential ingredients for a successful *polis* were an educated and engaged citizenry and a wise ruling class: Democracy combined with political aristocracy. Democracy with neither of these attributes would be a free but dangerously anarchic society whose lack of discipline made it easily susceptible to tyranny. To ward against such decay, his preferred form of government was led by a committee of public-spirited "Guardians." Today we call such a system *technocracy*. America has more than enough democracy. What it needs is more technocracy—a lot more.

The way to get there is ideally neither war nor revolution—nor a bout of tyranny—but to evolve America's political system in a more technocratic direction. Technocratic government is built around expert analysis and long-term planning rather than narrow-minded and short-term populist whims. Technocrats are *not* to be confused with the complacent establishment elites that were just stunned by Trump. Real technocracy has the virtues of being both utilitarian (inclusively seeking the broadest societal benefit) and meritocratic (with the most qualified and non-corrupt leaders). Instead of *ad hoc* and reactive politics, technocracies are where political *science* starts to look like something worthy of the term: A rigorous approach to policy.

Technocracies are more IQ test than popularity contest: The percentage of social mindshare governed by petty politics is far reduced. In technocratic regimes one doesn't hear phrases like "learn on the fly" or "rely on your advisors." They don't indulge in short-term political circus acts such as the "First 100 Days." Rather than fact-free debates, data and democracy have equal value in guiding strategy. Technocracies also don't waste time with ideologically stale dichotomies such as "big" versus "small" government, but think issue-by-issue about how government can be most useful.

Sound good to you? You're not alone. The most recent World Values Survey reveals that from World War II to today, the percentage of people in Europe and the US who feel it is "essential to live in a democracy" has fallen from two-thirds to under one-third. Meanwhile, the proportion of Americans who believe that experts should decide what is best for the country rather than the government has risen from 32% to 49%.

In other words: Americans are craving a better government—one that balances democracy and technocracy.

Unfortunately, America today suffers from an abundance of representation and a deficit of administration. There is a great excess in the power of representatives—congressmen and senators—and deep shortfall in the power of administrators—governors and mayors. There are too many officials trained in law and not enough in policy: In other words, too much time spent arguing rather than doing something. If the same political chaos that brought the Founding Fathers together in 1787 is present today, then it is again time for a new constitutional convention.

This short book is a background memo for that process, a combination of what we know and what we can imagine about designing an effective government that serves the people. The first two sections bring you up to speed on the latest thinking on what constitutes good governance with a spotlight on two countries, one the world's most genuine democracy and the other the most admired technocracy, as well as a tour of what we can learn from how well these and other small states are run. The latter three sections then apply these findings to construct the ideal 21st century political system for America.

American democracy could be made far more effective through the technocratic toolkit being deployed around the world in better-run countries. There are three things that the best governments do well: Respond efficiently to citizens' needs and preferences, learn from international experience in devising policies, and use data and scenarios for long-term planning. If done right, such governments marry the virtues of democratic inclusiveness with the effectiveness of technocratic management.

The ideal type of government that results is what I call a *direct technocracy*.

In America, direct technocracy would look like this: A collective presidency of about a half-dozen committee members backed by a strong civil service better able to juggle complex challenges; a multi-party legislature better reflective of the diversity of political views and using data technologies for real-time citizen consultation, and the Senate replaced by a Governors Assembly that prioritizes the common needs of states and shares successful policies across them; and a judicial branch that monitors international benchmarks and standards, and proposes constitutional amendments to keep pace with our rapidly changing times.

Some of these proposals may seem unrealistic given our present institutions and politics—but history punishes societies that don't evolve. Tocqueville came from beyond our shores in praise of America's embodiment of progressive political ideals. Today Americans should travel beyond their own shores in search of inspiration.

1.
EVOLUTION OF AN ARCHETYPE

The Secret to Success

The most publicly minded efforts are sometimes held in deep secrecy. Each year, at an exclusive spa resort in the Alps, a private family foundation gathers the most influential figures from Swiss politics, business, and academia to debate the issues of the day and devise roadmaps for economic initiatives, diplomatic relations, urban planning projects, and other national priorities. On hand at the gathering in early 2014 were the speaker of the parliament, heads of all political parties, cabinet advisors, newspaper publishers, chiefs of private banks, prominent scholars from sciences and humanities, and a couple of foreign guests. After a few hours of presentations and small group brainstorming surrounded by flipcharts busily filled with boxes and arrows, it was time for each table to read out its analysis and recommendations. As the discussion carried on, one senior parliamentary figure grew impatient. "Where is the creativity in any of this? We came here to blow up our complacency," he admonished. "I want to see some quantum leaps!"

Rarely is a national elite so tough on itself—and yet if any country deserves to pat itself on the back, it's Switzerland, which sits at or near the top of nearly every global index of wealth, competitiveness, quality of life, innovation, and many other indicators. But Switzerland's cardinal virtue is self-reliance. Precisely because it is small and vulnerable, it has been fiercely protective of its independence and neutrality throughout Europe's turbulent centuries. It was home to the League of Nations in the early 20th century and hosts the second headquarters of the United Nations—but only actually joined the UN itself in 2002. It sits in the middle of the European Union, but will probably never join it. The rallying cry I heard multiple times at the 2014 retreat was "Integrieren heisst verlieren!" ("To integrate is to capitulate," or more colloquially interpreted: "Integration is for losers.")

The strategic paranoia that animates Swiss leadership is shared by at least one other country—the one chosen as the special guest nation at the 2014 Alpine gathering: Singapore. Switzerland and Singapore are the only two countries in the world that rank in the top tier across all the following indices that suggest having a real plan for the future: The WEF's Global Competitiveness Index, Infrastructure Quality Index, and Sustained Prosperity Index, INSEAD's Global Innovation Index, and the World Bank's Government Effectiveness Index. These two small states have become global standard bearers for health and wealth, low corruption and high employment.

On the surface, few countries could seem more different than Switzerland and Singapore. They are both roughly shaped like horizontal diamonds and have red-and-white colored flags, but the similarities end there. Switzerland is a 700-year-old European democracy while Singapore is an Asian technocracy that turned 50 in 2015. Switzerland is the epitome of bottom-up democracy:

Local plebiscites influence even strategic national decisions; the national interest cannot deviate from the popular will of the people. Switzerland is so decentralized it does not have a president (or head of state), but rather a Federal Council of seven members whose chairman rotates each year. (Most citizens cannot name even three of the seven.)

Singapore, by contrast, has become synonymous with top-down, government-knows-best rule. Policies have historically been designed by technocrats outside of public scrutiny. Singapore's founding father Lee Kuan Yew micro-managed the country for 40 years, and his son Lee Hsien Loong is the current prime minister. (Everyone knows their names.) Even the aesthetics are opposed: Switzerland is mountainous and landlocked; Singapore a tropical seaport. Singapore is a city-state; it is 100 percent urbanized. By contrast, one third of Switzerland's population is rural; the country is famous for snow-capped mountains and cows. Singapore's skyline features glistening corporate towers, while Switzerland's tallest building (the headquarters of pharmaceutical firm Roche in Basel) scarcely reaches forty stories (still far shorter than the country's tallest dam).

So which is the ideal system for a complex and fast-changing world? In which direction should today's haphazard Western democracies reform: Swiss-style popular democracy or Singapore-style strategic technocracy? What model should post-authoritarian or newly democratic societies pursue: Swiss-style organic economic diversification or Singapore-style managed innovation?

The answer is both. Having lived for stretches in both these small countries, I've come to see that despite their enormous differences, what matters most is that Switzerland and Singapore are *both* verifiably democratic *and* rigorously technocratic at the same time. They both have a high percentage of foreign-born populations, national military and civil service, strong linkages between education and industry, diversified economies, and massive state investment in R&D and innovation.

A hybrid of Swiss direct democracy and Singaporean technocracy—*a direct technocracy*—is the superior form of government for the 21st century.[1] Indeed, if Plato were alive today, he would select the educated and activist Swiss populace as his ideal citizens and Singapore's rigorously trained technocrats as the chosen "Guardians." A hybrid of the two would be world's most boring but effective regime—precisely what every country should aspire to. It does not matter that these are small countries with vastly different histories from America. There is no one universal political model for the world—neither America's nor theirs—but all large countries could evolve towards better governance by studying Switzerland and Singapore's marriage of democracy and data.

---

1 In the 2009 novel *Forever Pleasure*, Theodore Eastmann describes a direct technocracy as "a form of government designed to give all human being equal opportunities for the highest quality of life."

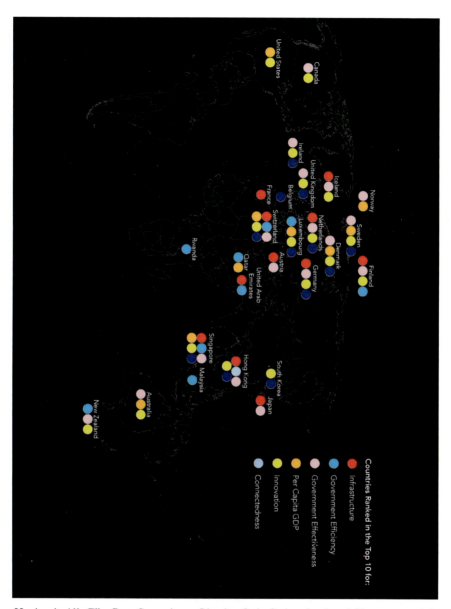

Having it All: The Best Countries to Live in. Only Switzerland and Singapore rank in the top ten across a wide range of measurements of quality of life and good governance.

For a high-res version of this infographic, please visit:
http://www.paragkhanna.com/home/2016/10/18/technocracy-in-america

PARAG KHANNA

A New State for a New Era

The search for an ideal state form best suited to the times is not an idle philosophical exercise but a recurrent necessity. Today most governments lack the capacity to do anything more than react incoherently to events. America's financial wizardry both caused its financial crisis while also bailing itself out from it, but beyond the numbers the human cost in social dislocation, deferred retirement, and loss of national morale has been devastating. Even European welfare states have been shell-shocked by the ripple effects, with Greece and Spain experiencing mass unemployment, crippling austerity, and people forced to beg in the street and rummage through trash for food. Then there are the growing risks of geopolitical confrontation and cyber-war, transnational terrorist and criminal groups, economic competition and protectionism, climate change and natural disasters, and technological disruptions to our everyday way of life. No society can let its guard down for even a second.

Over the past seventy years, scholars have endeavored to identify the regime type best suited to the conditions of the times. In the early 1940s, Yale political scientist Harold Lasswell hailed the rise of "garrison states" such as America and Japan, where elites governed the military-industrial complex necessary to prevail in World War II and the Cold War. But strength alone is insufficient to delivery security and prosperity. Today the only countries we call "garrison states" are nuclear-armed failed states like North Korea.

As Cold War barriers dissolved, attention shifted towards how to capitalize on the onset of a truly global marketplace—a world of geoeconomics over geopolitics. Harvard Business School professor Michael Porter argued that achieving competitive advantage required building strategic clusters of industries to attract investment. Concentrating production, building interdependence, and investing in human capital—rather than expanding territory—would lead to the rise of what UCLA and Harvard economic historian Richard Rosecrance in 1996 labeled the "virtual state" or "trading state." Extending this emphasis on the economic over the political, Philip Bobbit, in his masterful *Shield of Achilles* (2003), traced the emergence of the "market state" era in which the maximization of individual commercial opportunity defines power and success. Lastly, business strategist Keniche Ohmae, in his book *The Next Global Stage* (2005), argued that urban agglomerations of city-states resembling the medieval Hanseatic League would become the world's power centers.

The search for an optimal state form continues into the information age—and it should logically be called the "Info-State." The info-state is an evolution and modification of these earlier models. Whereas Ohmae's model operated on just-in-time cycles, like Japanese corporations, and Rosecrance's was disaggregated like a laptop manufacturing supply chain, 21st century info-states don't fully trust the invisible hand of the free market. Instead the public and private sectors join forces to develop strategic economic master plans to maintain their edge. Switzerland and Singapore are geographically small, but their ability to concentrate and harness flows of money, goods, resources, technology, information and talent makes them gravitationally large. Their economic geography matters as much as their political geography: Indeed, they define their geography by their connectivity rather than just their territory; their supply chains are as important to their map as their location. At the same time, while they are the archetype of open economies, they also have fortress-like elements, always vigilant to control migration and filter out financial contagion, cyber-hackers and terrorists.

Info-states such as Switzerland and Singapore are also the places where we can witness the best efforts at *direct technocracy*. Rather than governing by staggered electoral mandates alone, they also practice real-time consultation with citizens through plebiscites and petitions, surveys and public workshops. The info-state is thus a postmodern democracy (or "post-democracy") that combines popular priorities with technocratic management. Experiments in direct technocracy are already visible around the world from Estonia and Israel to the UAE and Rwanda to India and China—across both democracies and non-democracies. Info-state governments therefore don't toe one agenda; their mandate is to always improve in all areas—no excuses. Their only ideology is pragmatism.

As with natural selection, governance models evolve over time through adaptation, modification, and imitation. The more the world becomes connected and complex, devolved and data-saturated, the more the info-state model will rise in status. Global political discourse is shifting into a post-ideological terrain where performance—based on citizen satisfaction and international benchmarks—is the arbiter of success. All societies want a balance of prosperity and livability, openness and protection, effective governance and citizen voice, individualism and cohesion, free choice and social welfare. Everyday people don't measure these things by how "democratic" their state is but whether they feel safe in their cities, can afford their homes, have stability in their work, have a plan for growing old, and can remain connected to friends and family. Comparing countries by GDP per capita alone has been reduced to statistical sophistry compared to these more tangible aspects of quality of life. Instead, we are coming to appreciate that the difference between successful and failing countries today is not rich versus poor, left versus right, or democratic versus authoritarian, but whether they have the capacity to meet their citizens' basic needs, empower them as individuals, and act or change course when needed. Everything else is window dressing.

For America, this means taking a hard look in the mirror and realizing that the days of moralizing condescension are over—ironically, claiming you're the best precisely because you don't know any better. Tocqueville warned of Americans' tendency towards "perpetual self-adoration." But the presumption that America's political system is better than the rest is giving way to the realization that other systems are categorically better, and America needs to learn from them.

Beyond Democracy to Good Governance

The spread of democracy has hit many stumbling blocks since the end of the Cold War. Self-inflicted wounds are the primary cause: Populism has hijacked governments from Argentina to Hungary, strongman nationalism has usurped Russia, Turkey and Venezuela, coups and corruption have stymied Pakistan, Nigeria, and other states. According to Stanford professor Larry Diamond, the rate of "democracy breakdown" has doubled during the 1999-2011 period over the 1986-1998 years. Freedom House's 2014 report finds that 54 countries show declining political and civil rights. The majority of the world's countries are still nominally electoral democracies—but the more democracies there are, the more they give democracy a bad name.

The term "democracy" tells us ever less about how—or how well—a country is run. Indeed, from Mexico to Italy, democracies today are the places where surveys show populations having the least trust and respect for politicians. In countries like Iran and Russia, elections are merely instruments of pacification, a release valve that buys breathing space for regimes.² Rule of law, meaning laws are above the executive, looks more like rule *by* law, in which governments abuse the law as a tool of power. More than half of Russians believe Putin's ruling party is full of "crooked thieves." In Brazil, the rising middle class has rebelled against a democratically elected but incompetent kleptocracy. Democratic elections alone are clearly insufficient to ensure accountable governance.

In Asia too, democracy is more an exercise in vote-banking than political progress. The world's most populous democracy, India, has long embodied the phenomenon of elections as auctions, an elaborate yet unsophisticated arms race to buy votes (particularly along ethnic lines) with sacks of rice or flat-screen TVs.³ Indian politics has in fact always been run by "family firms," in the words of scholar Ramachandra Guha. By 2013, former Indian Prime Minister Manmohan Singh's cabinet had grown to 28 members as the Congress party added ministers from key electoral states to curry favor with voters. The Congress Party, once the august backbone of Indian politics, has devolved into a back-bench mob run by an Italian matriarch and her bumbling son. In Bangladesh, too, democracy is an endless poker game

---

2   Scholars Steven Levitsky and Lucan Way have aptly named this phenomenon "competitive authoritarianism," in which democratically elected regimes use government powers to weaken opposition and cement their position.

3   See Kanchan Chandra, *Why Ethnic Parties Succeed: Patronage and Ethnic Headcounts in India*. Cambridge: Cambride University Press, 2004.

amongst two ruling families who use control over ministries and courts to undermine each other at every turn—agreeing only to pass laws that curb judicial independence and press freedom.

This—not the vision of America's Founding Fathers—is the reality of "democracy" for most of the world's population that lives in nominally democratic states. Few people in these countries are under any illusions that their democracies are well functioning, so nor should Americans be.

Imagine you are the incoming president of a young populous Asian nation emerging from colonialism or dictatorship—let's call it Asiana. Which state would you aspire to replicate: China or India? Singapore or the Philippines? Vietnam or Indonesia? Across Asia, people look at the democracies of India, Indonesia and the Philippines (whose combined population is nearly 1.7 *billion* people) with a mix of pity and hope: Pity that they are such poor and poorly governed countries, and hope that they get their act together and run themselves like Asia's better-managed technocracies—which means not just Singapore but even Malaysia, Vietnam and Thailand. Malaysia is mired in corruption but is stable, modern multi-ethnic state with first-world infrastructure and rising prosperity. Vietnam is a single-party regime yet has massively modernized the country and reduced poverty, with foreign investment pouring in to employ its hard-working and skilled population. Thailand's 2014 coup ousted incompetent democratic leaders in favor of a military junta; Thais backed a permanent political role for the military in a constitutional referendum in 2016. These aren't ideal regimes, but they're orders of magnitude superior to Bangladesh or Indonesia.

It is precisely because India, Indonesia and the Philippines have each endured decades of forgettable or regrettable governments that they have all in recent years elected leaders with explicitly *technocratic* pretensions. Indians, Indonesians and Filipinos are no longer content to be part of vibrant commercial societies but with dysfunctional governments. Fed up with patronizing clichés about how they thrive despite their governments, they have voted in governments with no-nonsense agendas focused on infrastructure, jobs, education and technology.

Here then is a key reason to pay attention to technocracy: Because it is Asia's future. Technocracy becomes a form of salvation after societies realize that democracy doesn't guarantee national success. Democracy eventually gets sick of itself and votes for technocracy. Think about it: These three countries have had functional democracy for at least a generation, but only now is the world paying attention to their progress in digital ID cards, cutting red tape, and establishing special economic zones—all ideas that come from technocratic leaders. Because East Asian societies are modern and increasingly liberal, they will evolve towards better governance that balances political openness with goal-oriented technocracy.

The rise of elected technocrats comes not a moment too soon for Asia's masses. India's Narendra Modi and Indonesia's Joko Widodo have backgrounds as provincial governors where they confronted local needs and tested ideas. They are a reminder that leaders with actual experience governing are almost always a superior choice to representative politicians—and also that poor non-elite leaders can aspire to be good technocrats. Indeed, it is well known that while Modi rode democracy to the top, he is a "tea stall technocrat." He has no patience for trite rubbish such as the "First 100 Days," and declared a national day of mourning in India when Lee Kuan Yew passed away in 2015.

Western political commentators presume that good technocrats will eventually be replaced by bad ones—the "bad emperor" problem—sending countries back to the drawing board with democracy's primacy restored. But the last thing India needs is more American-style democratic rancor. The difference in India's and China's regimes—and in their performance—over the past fifty years proves beyond any doubt that it is market capitalism—rather than democracy—that drives growth, and government capacity that enables welfare delivery. As INSEAD dean Ilian Mihov has demonstrated through correlating variables of the World Bank's Worldwide Governance Indicators (WGI) to economic growth, it is rule of law that ultimately correlates to success, not democracy.[4]

What India's new technocrats realize is that, unlike China, India went through political devolution prior to building national unity, meaning it remains much less than the sum of its parts. Successive governments have perennially made pay-outs to the provinces to purchase loyalty, which only encouraged further fragmentation. At independence, India had only 14 provinces; today it has 29. Modi is not out to reverse democracy but to compensate for this debilitating sequence of devolution before modernization by spending $150 billion on railways, pushing through a national goods and services tax, and launching campaigns to prioritize toilets over temples. For all his flaws, his technocratic mantra is a big step forward for India: "Minimum government, maximum governance."

---

4 The World Bank's Worldwide Governance Indicators (WGI) rank countries according to metrics grouped into six categories: Voice and Accountability, Political Stability, Government Effectiveness, Regulatory Quality, Rule of Law, and Control of Corruption.

In western thought, a deep complacency has set in that confuses politics with governance, democracy with delivery, process with outcomes. But the "will of the people" is not just to repeat their desires over and over without results. China's spectacular rise versus that of democracies such as India has shown the world that it is better to have a system focused on delivery without democracy than a system that is too democratic at the expense of delivery. For democracy to be admired, it has to deliver. Elections are an instrument of accountability, not a mode of delivery. The input legitimacy of democracy can never compensate for the output legitimacy of delivering the basics.

Good technocracies are equally focused on inputs and outputs. Their legitimacy comes both from the process by which the government is selected and the delivery of what citizens universally proclaim they want: Solid infrastructure, public safety, clean air and water, reliable transportation, ease of doing business, good schools, quality housing, dependable childcare, freedom of expression, access to jobs, and so on. The technocratic mindset is that delay in getting these things done is itself a form of corruption. Instead of perpetual blame games and acceptance of stasis as the norm, good technocracies are always out to solve their problems.

Once we stop preaching democracy and instead ask what is the essential course for governments to get their act together and stop inflicting unnecessary suffering on their people, we can move from style to substance. In the long run, the quality of governance matters more than regime type. And with good governance comes trust. Singaporeans have very high trust in their public institutions because they are both effective and non-corrupt. As Tom Friedman has put it, "Singapore is not a full democracy, but its leaders ask each day how to make the country better. If institutions are in place and the government is perceived as just, then democracy is optional." Actually Singapore has called itself a "democracy of deeds" since the 1960s, and more recently a "problem-solving democracy."

At the same time, neither Singapore nor China makes any apologies for achieving success despite not mimicking Western models. Why would they when today it is citizens of democracies who clamor for technocracy more than the citizens of technocracies demand more democracy? Indeed, some of the strongest advocates of Chinese-style long-term, top-down economic policy-making are to be found in democratic South Africa and India. After all, the average person in "communist" China leads a far better life in almost every possible dimension than the average person in "democratic" India. Chinese citizens not surprisingly also trust their government far more than their Indian counterparts. As one Chinese scholar has said, "Chinese people don't love their government, but they trust it."

Let's take away from all of this not that democracy is undesirable, for it is not only a crucial foundation of legitimacy, but also a vital pillar of successful technocracy. Instead, democracy has to be seen not as a universal solution but a principle to be observed in the quest towards the higher objective of good governance. The elements of good governance—accountable leadership, national stability, political inclusion, effective service delivery, regulatory quality, transparent rule of law, low corruption, impartial judiciary, civil liberties, protection of rights, provision of economic opportunity and other variables—are proferred by all modern societies. America is hardly unique in enshrining them. What matters is execution as measured by the process for determining laws, the autonomy of the bureaucracy, and the effectiveness of policy delivery, among other metrics.

Successful governments are also differentiated by their capacity to adapt to rapidly changing conditions. Good governance requires grasping complex global trends and developing far-sighted strategy with accelerated decision-making—none of which democracy itself excels at providing. Technocrats of the past have been accused of failing to cope with complexity; today it is the democracies that are failing to adjust to new realities. Indeed, today's technocratic regimes bear little resemblance to those associated with the term a generation or two ago. They are not Mao's cult of personality or Soviet central planning. They are civil rather than military, inclusive rather than a clique, data-driven rather than dogmatic, and more transparent than opaque. Even the world's oldest democracy is more technocratic than you think.

2.
HOW TO RUN A COUNTRY

Switzerland: Too Small to Fail

One of the world's oldest continuous republics, the confederacy of cantons that comprises Switzerland has practiced direct democracy since 1291. The 18th century philosopher Jean-Jacques Rousseau argued that direct democracy made the Swiss the world's happiest people, one of the many indicators Switzerland tops alongside Norway, New Zealand and other small countries. Since the 26 cantons banded together in 1848 to form the Swiss confederation, over half of all the plebiscites that have taken place in the world have been in Switzerland. In any village the bright orange signs are unmistakeable: "Heute Abstimmung!" ("Vote today!") Communities convene and deliberate as often as twice per month on matters such as public spending, and have quarterly balloting for cantonal and national initiatives and referenda. Voter turnout is a healthy 50 percent, and higher for more significant or controversial issues.

The Swiss government trusts the people but also empowers them. The Swiss will soon vote on lowering the voting age to 16 (which one canton already allows). Civic education and financial literacy are not outsourced only to schools; people learn by doing.

Direct democracy exposes differences and acrimony, but it also builds trust; they cannot blame the government for their own decisions. "The Swiss no longer believe in churches and religion," muses Reto Steiner, a professor at the University of Bern. "They put their trust in deliberation, academics and experts. Consultants are too expensive," he chuckles.

Swiss are not hostage to outdated and subjective constitutional provisions such as America's second amendment. With only 100,000 signatures, Swiss citizens can also instigate national initiatives to propose new laws and even constitutional amendments, or referenda to challenge them.[5] The parliament can vote to discourage the population and the Federal Council can also make dissuading statements, but the people ultimately decide. The Swiss citizens' will holds even if their sentiments go against existing constitutional provisions. For example, in 2009 the Swiss banned the construction of minarets, which goes against the constitution's protection of the freedom of expression. The Swiss are also not opposed to promoting initiatives that are hostile to capitalist orthodoxy. Several recent campaigns—to massively curb "fat cat" executive compensation to no more than twelve times that of junior employees, to end the country's wealth-friendly flat tax, to ban the sale of gold by the central bank, and to set the world's highest minimum wage ($25 per hour)—all failed narrowly, but sent a signal that even with their reputation as a tax haven domiciling one-quarter of Europe's top-paid CEOs, the Swiss believe they can compete on a fairer playing field.

Switzerland is not just politically but also socially inclusive.

---

5 German and Italian voters increasingly show a preference for electing parliamentary candidates who promise direct democracy and opportunities for referenda.

No country spends more per capita on healthcare and education. Switzerland's healthcare system is entirely privatized, yet 100 percent of the country buys it, with the government only subsidizing the cost for the poorest. Universal coverage costs only 3.5% of GDP, while the US spends 8.5% and only less than 80% of the population has coverage.

With Switzerland's cantonal system of distributed taxation and budgeting, financial stress in one part of the country doesn't have a domino effect on the rest. Even as Switzerland personifies stable democracy, make no mistake that it is highly technocratic. A highly educated caste of professional bureaucrats devotes decades-long careers to overseeing a consistent tax policy, ensuring that the sacrosanct rule of law applies to everyone, and managing the country's world-class infrastructure—making sure the trains run like clockwork. Not only the government but also the workforce is highly technocratic: Trained, competent and productive workers who virtually never go on strike. Democracy doesn't deliver Switzerland's perfectionist efficiencies; technocracy does.

Even the world's best democracy actually knows very well that democracy is insufficient to cope with complexity. Indeed, Professor Steiner worries that Switzerland's reputation for high-standards and efficiency is slipping—evidenced by its slide in the World Bank's "Doing Business" ranking while Singapore tops the list. Now it is Singapore that runs with the precision of a Swiss watch. To stave off the crisis of confidence many other western democracies are suffering, its leading practitioner is therefore studying Singapore to see how it can evolve to the next level.

Singapore: From Consent to Consultation

Lee Kuan Yew, Singapore's constant gardener, was fond of saying that it is more important to be correct than politically correct. He believed the phrase "law and order" has the terms reversed: Order matters first and foremost, then law. In its early years, Singapore's town hall meetings featured Chinese, Tamils and Malays bickering at each other in their own languages, so Lee Kuan Yew imposed English. Bandits used to kidnap and extort both locals and foreigners; Lee Kuan Yew made it punishable by death. Singaporean society has become more even ethnically diverse; reckless abuses of liberty such as inciting communal hatred, even in the name of "free speech," are a senseless luxury at best and self-destructive at worst. Together with his deputies such as Goh Keng Swee, Lee set about rebuilding British-style government root and branch. Success, not pandering to Western archetypes, made him one of the 20th century's most universally admired statesmen—and his country a role model for would-be info-states in the 21st century.

Given this history, it is no surprise that Singapore sought to institutionalize technocracy before democracy. Too much politics corrupts democracy, and too much democracy gets in the way of policy. Politics is about positions, policy about decisions; democracies produce compromises, technocracies produce solutions; democracy satisfices, technocracy optimizes. Some caricature Singapore as Tocqueville's "good despotism," a regime that seeks to provide for all the people's gratifications and "spare them all the care of thinking and all the trouble of living." But a proper technocracy is much more flexible than that. Lee Kuan Yew originally had socialist pretensions before pivoting in the 1970s to more Hong Kong-style flexible labor markets. China too has shifted from the radical universal dogmatism of Mao to the incremental pragmatism of Deng, whose accrued experiments resulted in China's economic miracle. Modern technocracy does not seek to suffocate, though it is capable of both large-scale "shock therapy" as well as small-scale iterative experimentation.

Paradoxes thus appear that make perfect sense in practice—if not in theory. Singapore can be described as freewheeling—it has no trade restrictions, is the easiest place to start a business, and prostitution is legal—but also as a nanny state: It has the world's most robust government-subsidized private home ownership scheme[6], mandatory savings for retirement[7], and a universal and cost-effective public healthcare system. It is a top-ranked free market yet the government manages 60 percent of the economy through state-backed companies. In other words, it is a libertarian nanny-state where capitalist self-reliance fuses with redistributive hand-outs to raise the incomes of the bottom ten percent[8]. It is big government, but also lean and effective government.

Especially in the more than one hundred countries of the

---

6   Singapore's Housing Development Board (HDB) is an example of the government backing market mechanisms to achieve social goals. All qualified citizens are allotted their own condo to own based on their neighborhood and family size, but the cost and payment plan is tailored so that owners don't have to pay more than one-fourth of their monthly income (the lowest housing cost-to-income ratio of any advanced country). This one set of policies simultaneously ensures a roof over everyone's head, prevents predatory lending, and guarantees inter-generational wealth transfer through real estate ownership—all in one of the most land-scarce countries in the world.

7   Singapore's Central Provident Fund (CPF) requires that each citizen attain a savings level of about $125,000 by the age of 55 through a combination of employer and employee contributions. Contrast this with the US, where 60 percent of American workers have saved less than $25,000 for retirement, and 36 percent of baby boomers and retirees have effectively no savings at all.

8   In the past generation, 14 percent of the bottom 20 percent of families have risen into the top 20 percent in Singapore, double the rate of Americans that have experienced such upward mobility, and higher even than Denmark or Canada.

post-colonial world, the lack of succession planning makes them their own biggest threat. Singapore, however, has managed succession such that the passing of the nation's founder has not rocked the national boat. For all his dominance of national decision-making, Lee Kuan Yew explicitly decreed in his will that his modest home be razed to the ground so as not to become any kind of shrine. It is Lee Kuan Yew-*ism* that survives with its emphasis on non-corrupt meritocratic governance, infrastructure investment, an educated populace, and long-range planning. The average age of cabinet members has steadily come down, assuring both fresh blood and continuity of quality leadership.

This is the kind of thinking we are accustomed to seeing in successful corporations such as Royal Dutch Shell, which over decades has excelled at producing long-term, multi-disciplinary scenarios fusing trends in energy, geopolitics and technology. For this reason, Lee Kuan Yew decided to model Singapore's strategic planning on Shell itself. Scenarios are neither predictions nor straight-line projections, but are composites of emergent patterns that could combine into an integrated picture. In their bare-knuckled brainstorming sessions, Singaporeans constantly think about the future in terms of plausible scenarios that pull them far out of their comfort zone, and develop strategies to maintain their relevance. Scenario-led thinking reduces the emotional tension of policy debates, creating a safe space for disagreement over hypotheticals. Scenarios help to check the potential over-confidence of technocratic regimes by presenting challenging alternative narratives—the downside that one must always take into account. Andy Grove of Intel famously said, "Only the paranoid survive." The same is true of countries. No wonder Singapore is often described as the "world's best run company."

But it is also a think-tank, with scenario planners embedded in every ministry covering both domestic and international issues. These "foresight officers" organize and impartially frame scenarios for leaders to consider on an ongoing basis. For example, the Risk Assessment and Horizon Scanning (RAHS) program, while housed in the national security division, covers trends and drivers that affect all aspects of government planning from investment and budgeting to education and training. In the prime minister's office, the Centre for Strategic Futures (CSF) aggregates these scenarios and publishes analysis and commentary on them in its own high-quality journal, *Future Tense*.

Governing through scenarios is not just for policy wonks. In Singapore it's an inclusive societal undertaking that draws on widely distributed knowledge. The PRISM process of the National University's Institute for Policy Studies (IPS) was a multi-year public consultation that crowd-sourced insights from hundreds of experts and citizens to build realistic scenarios for the Singapore of 2022 such as "SingaStore," in which the government balances its pro-business orientation with a preference for high-wage jobs for Singaporeans, or "WikiCity," in which the government reduces its role to purely legal and external functions while a proactive citizenry manages the economic and social marketplace.[9]

Even strategic long-term questions are aired systematically with the population. Over the course of 2013, the "Our Singapore Conversation" process convened 660 dialogues with over 47,000 participants, surveyed 4,000 more citizens, and partnered with

---

9   Gillian Koh, "Singapore's Political Transition," *Global-is-Asian*, Jan-Mar 2013.

40 different NGOs to collect views. Dialogues were conducted in seven languages and even held overseas in London, San Francisco, Shanghai and Beijing to capture the concerns of the diaspora. OSC resulted in significant ideas ranging from requiring foreigners and women to partake in national service to redesigning public housing for the aging "silver tsunami" to giving individuals more control over their pension investment allocations. Similarly, in 2015 Singapore launched a Committee on the Future Economy (CFE) to map out the country's path towards adopting new industries and training its students and workforce accordingly. Anchored in the civil service, the process involved every ministry, dozens of domestic and foreign executives, and hundreds of academics and technology experts. In a high-tech version of Switzerland's referendum model, Singapore also launched a platform for online petitions (called "GoPetition") and established a parliamentary committee to derive recommendations from them. In all of these cases, recommendations are acted on within months, not years (or never).

Furthermore, all of these are examples of inclusive deliberation, though not a replica of Switzerland's direct democracy. The difference is crucial, for Singapore's leadership does not over-consult. Deliberation never degenerates into paralysis. Instead, governments set reasonable key performance indicators ("KPIs") that are tracked at regular intervals to assess progress. In no other society is the efficient delivery of public services so diligently monitored through KPIs. The SingPass system puts all government functions within reach online, and digital "jukeboxes" in government offices print out passports and other official documents so citizens don't have to wait on line. Home financing and re-financing can be arranged in a day. From passport checks and public toilets at the airport to banks and university administration buildings, Singapore is populated with little touchscreen iPads asking you to rate the service you've received—and the government actually pays attention to the results.

Singapore doesn't do foresight because it has more economists or money than America, but because its leaders have some capacity for autonomous, long-term decision-making and enjoy the trust of the public. In short-term-oriented electoral democracy, the future has no constituency; everything has to be "sold" to the people as a quick high. It is precisely because, as the political psychologist Philip Tetlock has demonstrated, full transparency over political deliberations can lead to decisions that are aimed at being popular rather than correct, that democracy must be tempered with technocratic instruments that assess the long-term implications of decisions and offer correctives. Tetlock's work also famously demonstrates the failure of so-called experts to correctly predict a range of political and economic events. This is not a knock on technocracy. Governance is not about predictions but decisions. Technocrats aren't supposed to compete in prediction markets but listen to them, as well as to subject-matter experts and the public, and craft holistic policy. Being self-correcting is more important than being correct in any one thing.

Singapore itself is not immune from miscalculating the consequences of certain policies. Discouraging car ownership through electronic road pricing (ERP), which Singapore pioneered in the 1990s, failed to reduce congestion because it was underpriced vis-à-vis using the country's public transportation network. At the same time, between 2001-2011, Singapore allowed in about one million new residents from mainland China, India and elsewhere, while also allowing foreigners to buy into public housing, creating both a housing squeeze and price surge that angered many locals. Not surprisingly, when the government's Population White Paper was released, it unleashed major acrimony as many citizens feared the swelling foreign population. The backlash was felt in the 2011 election when Singapore's dominant People's Action Party (PAP) was caught off guard and lost half a dozen parliamentary seats to the Workers Party. Suddenly the PAP was no longer trusted by default.

That 2011 election sparked a major transition from governance by consent to governance through consultation. While initially difficult to swallow, a culture of consultation has come to be seen not as paternalism but professionalism, a shift from government-knows-best to crowdsourcing. This is a healthy source of political dynamism. Today every government agency conducts frequent public consultations on things people care about: Subway fares, car insurance rates, annuities for the elderly, and tax breaks for small and medium-sized enterprises. During the 2013 budget debate, parliamentarians held real-time dialogues with citizen groups on specific provisions. Every bill before the parliament has a public comment period.

It's important to note, however, that social media has as much to do with this evolution in Singaporean governance as the rise of alternative parties. Even if the Workers Party had not scored surprising gains in the 2011 parliamentary elections, citizens now openly challenge the government—online, at public forums, through the courts, and at the Speakers Corner in Hong Lim Park—on major issues such as the returns on pension fund investments, the timing of elections and immigration policy. Singaporeans complain relentlessly and demand results, a very different culture from emotive but fruitless protests witnessed regularly in other advanced societies.

Governance is more than a branch of operations research; society is a complex organism, not a washing machine. It is not just managing people and delivering them services but actively consulting and representing them. By the time of the 2015 election, the PAP had so studiously absorbed and coopted the Workers Party agenda and insights from scenario-building and public consultations that it won in a landslide. Modernization theory posits that with growing wealth and stability, political systems will become more pluralistic, featuring greater opposition and diversity of parties. Indeed, as Singaporean scholar Gillian Koh has pointed out, "People of wealthier social-economic status want to have opposition for its own sake as a check and balance." But Singapore's population did just the opposite, reducing the opposition to only a single seat. They are not interested in politics for the sake of it—only in results.

Still, the more Singapore liberalizes, the less "safe seats" there are. Activists are emerging as national political figures, and individuals can run for office on independent platforms. Seats are guaranteed for Non-Constituency Members of Parliament (NCMP), all of whom come from opposition ranks, and there are 9 independent Nominated Members of Parliament (NMPs) chosen for their independent stature and authority in the fields of education, business, philanthropy or sports. It matters less how many seats the opposition occupies than that Singapore is now a place where all voices are heard....almost.

Dissent is crucial to any society's success. It brings an essential perspective on what is not going right and a valuable downside scenario of what could go wrong in the future. Allowing public dissent, whether films on regrettable historical episodes or bloggers who challenge the government, is as important as having mechanisms for whistleblowers to report on corruption and abuse of power. For decades the PAP has continued to proffer the narrative of geopolitical vulnerability that surrounded the country's early years, conditions that have long passed. So too has the need for out-of-touch laws such as the criminalization of homosexuality or curtailed press freedoms. These are habits of a paranoid survivalist state, but they don't contribute to national resilience.

Donald Low, one of the most outspoken voices to emerge from inside the establishment, argues that Singapore has to learn to balance its knack for social engineering with the realities of social transition. While welfare states are being dismantled in the West, Low argues Singapore should deploy its ample budget surplus to towards greater spending on healthcare, housing, and social services to maintain a decent standard of living for all, preserving solidarity despite high inequality and growing diversity.

Europe's welfare states have ranked as the world's happiest societies for they have both material satisfaction and a sense of common purpose. Singapore has improved in the happiness rankings, earning the top spot in Asia in 2015, but its people are still considered less happy than Europeans, likely because of a combination of paranoia, ambition, and perpetual search for greater satisfaction. For generations Singaporeans have been told nobody owes them anything; they must be self-sufficient to survive. Having worked tirelessly to build a hyper-modern and secure enclave, they continue to see uncertainty everywhere in the form of rising living costs and competition from other regional hubs. To meet these challenges, the government stops at nothing to up the country's game, moving beyond just measuring technical results (through-put) towards capturing less tangible but equally important benefits (output). Graduating growing numbers of engineers is an example of the former, while making young Singaporeans hungry to innovate in creative industries represents the latter. They're also copying happiness-inducing policies from around the world: Free museum entry (as in London), free morning metro rides (as in Melbourne), greater care for the elderly (as in Denmark), and more education opportunities (as in Finland).

Singapore is forging a consensus around how to leverage foreign investment and talent to build the nation's own skill-set, boosting productivity through imported technology and management know-how, in order to reduce the demand for foreigners and mitigate congestion, inequality and social tension.[10] The back-and-forth between government, opposition and civil society has led to novel innovations such as a "buildability" score for construction projects that includes a metric for using standards that reduce the need for imported labor. Singapore will likely benefit from this approach: Costs have risen so quickly that major foreign companies have begun to look elsewhere in the region to locate their staff; but with less immigration and lower property prices, they will stay longer.

Prime Minister Lee Hsien Loong remarked on how Singapore's politics has become messier: "It's a different generation, a different society, and the politics will be different. We have to work in a more open way. We have to accept more of the untidiness and the to-ing and fro-ing, which is part of normal politics." But Singapore now practices an intense form of policy consultation that should not be confused for normal politics—and

---

10   Linda Lim, "Slower Growth, Stronger Nation," *Global-is-Asian*, Jan-Mar 2013.

should strive at all costs to avoid becoming normal politics.

There is a slippery slope from technocratic consultation to democratic populism—and the former should never be sacrificed for the latter. Today no country can afford the kind of short-term, narrow-minded populism that targets electoral outcomes rather than national performance, and wastes months or years with "lame-duck" pre-election paralysis. The greatest risk to Singapore may indeed be over-democratization, the risk that debating minutia overwhelms decision, that endless political dialogue supplants the relentless pursuit of excellence. Obvious and essential investments such as more public housing are an ongoing necessity, not a pawn to score electoral points. Before Singapore's elections became competitive, first-class infrastructure was not a political issue—it should not be today either.

"Democracy needs to be taken in healthy doses," a long-term American expat in Singapore once told me. "Drink a glass or two, but not the whole bottle." Many countries are beginning to appreciate this variation on the age-old adage: All things in moderation.

Securing the Info-State – and Citizens From It

Both Switzerland and Singapore perpetually fear regional instability and foreign aggression, and are armed with the latest military hardware. Small societies with mandatory conscription for males (and sometimes females) worry much less than other nations about European anti-military malaise or America's deep civil-military divide in which a small fraction of society bears the brunt of the military burden. As the American journalist John

McPhee famously narrated in *La Place de la Concorde* Suisse, "Switzerland doesn't have an army—it is an army." Switzerland was occupied by Napoleon in 1798 and surrounded by Nazi Germany during World War II, when it mobilized within three days and shot down a dozen Luftwaffe planes violating its airspace. In 2013 it even considered deploying armored vehicles to protect its borders against a potential influx of southern European refugees due to the financial crisis.

If Switzerland is the "armed hedgehog," then Singapore is the "poisonous shrimp." The island of Singapore is so small it fits within the letter "o" of its own name on the map. Born of an unamicable expulsion from Malaysia in 1965 amidst racial riots and hostilities with Sukarno's Indonesia, the Singapore of Lee Kuan Yew immediately implemented an Israeli-inspired military service requirement and built an armed force that continuously maintains total aerial supremacy in its neighborhood. Like Switzerland's concept of "armed neutrality," Singapore's security doctrine implements a deft multi-alignment, maintaining good relations with all great powers rather than allying too closely with any of them. Both have built massive subterranean caverns for storing food, oil and other chemicals, and bunkers for military hardware and data centers. They know they ultimately depend on the goodwill of superpowers, but at the same time they are as prepared as any state can be for global network disruptions or a world of total chaos.

Public safety is a top priority for technocratic governments—even if they go about it in different ways. In Singapore, private gun ownership is inconceivable, while community vigilance and strong deterrence (in the form of capital punishment) make Singapore the safest large city in the world. Jocular Americans still jibe about Singapore's caning of an American punk in the 1990s for vandalism, but never stop to wonder how it came to be that Singapore has virtually zero crime and an utterly negligible incarceration rate. The Swiss model achieves similar results but with an approach that combines freedom with civic maturity. Switzerland has almost as many guns per capita as America and Yemen, yet the combination of a generations-old culture of patriotic self-defense (the spirit of America's second amendment), strict permit and registration requirements, and a ban on automatic weapons also make Switzerland one of the safest countries in the world.

What about data, the new frontier in national security? The combination of 9/11 and the growing ubiquity of communications technology enabled something of an accidental conspiracy, namely the reflex of governments, democratic or otherwise, to build themselves into surveillance states. Through the Electronic Communications Privacy Act (ECPA), US government has recruited or coopted telecoms and technology companies to provide—or sell for hundreds of millions of dollars—data for the National Security Agency (NSA) to mine. Hackers, otherwise intent on disrupting digital services, stealing data and exposing illegal practices, have also been lured into collaboration with government agencies. Their combined forces have resulted in an arms race of new systems that enable perpetual physical and digital monitoring of entire societies. Domain Awareness Systems (DAS) such as the one Microsoft has deployed in cooperation with the NYPD to use cameras and other sensors to detect abnormal activity and protect critical infrastructure such as subways and power grids. Fake cell phone towers known as "interceptors" or "stingrays" have appeared in dozens of states nationwide, capable of extracting data from cell phones. America's domestic surveillance programs have created a painful gap between what liberties democracy is supposed to guarantee and what federal authorities practice in the shadows.

How can a citizen-centric info-state differentiate itself from the growing ranks of stealth police states? As it leverages technology to enhance security, it should do so with individual protection as the top priority and with minimal secrecy. In a world where governments *can* collect all data, the key issue is what they are *allowed* to access.

For example, while Singapore's telecom regulatory body the InfoComm Development Authority (IDA) can track mobile phone data, the government self-limits the geographic radius it is allowed to access to 200 meters. In the pursuit of day-to-day safety, Singapore has joined New York City and London in widely deploying security cameras in public areas, but it has placed them prominently and visibly, announcing their locations in the major newspapers and media to establish universal awareness.

When it comes to data monitoring, the Swiss "CrimPC" law also heavily restricts police ability to conduct surveillance without judicial and legislative approval.[11] Swiss lawmakers are also standing up for their data privacy against the US: In the uproar surrounding Edward Snowden's revelations about NSA spying activities—which began during his time in Geneva where the US operated a major surveillance system in contravention of its bilateral assurances and in violation of Swiss law—the country may offer Edward Snowden asylum in order for him

---

11   Susan Freiwald and Sylvain Metille, "Reforming Surveillance Law: The Swiss Model," Berkeley Technology Law Journal, Vol. 28 (2013).

to testify about NSA activities. The activism of Swiss citizens may ultimately contribute significantly to protecting American citizens' individual rights.

Info-State as Innovation State

Info-states are opportunistic by design, making physical and economic master plans hand-in-hand such that infrastructure is adaptable for multiple uses. They align the central government, companies, and educational institutions to direct their collective energy towards building industries relevant to global supply chains. Silicon Valley, contrary to the lore of the accidental confluence of weather and venture capital, has had strategic direction at every turn. Stanford University aspired to serve the industries of the emerging west coast since the 1890s, and after World War II provided space for companies such as Varian Associates that made military radar equipment. In the 1950s it incubated the Valley's early semiconductor firms and computing giants such as Hewlett-Packard, while receiving financial support from Xerox PARC. By the late 1960s it became one of four nodes for the Defense Department's ARPANET. Many of America's pioneering innovations from nuclear power to the Internet to GPS have their origins in US government programs. If governments didn't support entrepreneurial innovation, San Jose would not sit atop the world's value chain today.

This reality is a far cry from the government-versus-private-sector mentality that poisons America's policy debates today. In an info-state, the government should be as risk-taking as the private sector—ideally with the two in partnership. Public backing can be crucial to private risk-taking, which in turn produces technologies that serve national interests. In recent decades, Japan and South Korea have successfully built large innovation clusters both through strategic planning and healthy domestic competition. Dutch technology pioneer Philips in Eindhoven, Netherlands, owns over 130,000 patents, while Korean conglomerate Samsung in Seoul, has almost 500,000 employees and posted 2014 revenues of $300 billion. There is no debate about whether government has a role in innovation but rather which roles at what stage.

No country today better keeps the key industries and companies, labor markets and the educational establishment in sync better than Switzerland, maintaining near full employment and a highly skilled and productive workforce trained for lucrative industries. On the surface, Switzerland's approach to economic master planning is not to have one. But in fact it is rather that everyone in Switzerland has a strategy because of the country's openness to ideas, entrepreneurial spirit and technically focused education. Watches and knives, pharmaceuticals and chocolate, precision tools and encrypted hardware—almost everything Switzerland makes is better than anything anyone else can offer. This is because rather than shun vocational education, Swiss overwhelmingly prefer apprenticeships as a mode of skill-building for the global marketplace. As of 2016, Swiss firms were even setting up vocational apprenticeships in the US in order to help the American population "up-skill" and become a more attractive investment destination. These deep historical and cultural foundations have made Switzerland the leading winner of Nobel prizes per capita.

Such conditions are not easy to replicate, but Singapore is trying to emulate Switzerland by promoting polytechnic education as a first-tier rather than second-tier option, and by creating "learning passports" that record educational and training experiences across the full spectrum of institutions, including online courses. It has partnered with regional industry associations to train Singaporeans in the next generation of professions such as data-driven logistics and infrastructure finance, and matched each of its vocational schools with a counterpart from Switzerland and Germany to acquire the best curricula across a range of fields. The top three most competitive economies in the world according to the Global Innovation Index (GII) are Switzerland, South Korea and Singapore, all of which have vocational educational systems and worker retraining programs and near-zero unemployment. In info-states, education is thus more than a campaign slogan; it's a national priority. Singapore's prime minister is a computer scientist, and both deputy prime ministers have been education minister. Like its technocrats, teachers in Singapore are respected and paid well, a telltale sign of an info-state.

America's unemployment benefits alone don't retrain workers for new jobs the way such vocational systems do. Meanwhile, European countries such as Denmark guarantee training positions for workers who have been unemployed for as little as four months. Danish workers laid off from closed shipyards have quickly transitioned into jobs with Vestas, the wind power giant. Furthermore, America's excessive shareholder capitalism has meant that its companies discount the costs of R&D and worker training to pad quarterly growth, while European companies make far higher investments in up-skilling, the result of corporate governance structures in which labor has seats on management boards. The price is slightly lower growth, but more egalitarian societies.

Countries without America's geographic size, depth of capital markets, generations of industrial innovation and scale of talent—which is every other country in the world—cannot afford to arbitrarily experiment with their industrial foundations until they get lucky. Instead, they have to determine their strategic niche and practice the seemingly paradoxical "managed innovation" the way Singapore does, targeting specific sectors (either low or high value) for which they can marry foreign capital and talent with local labor and logistics to build competitive advantage.

So-called innovation states also invest heavily in R&D. Eyeing the model of Switzerland and the Nordics, Singapore is boosting its R&D expenditure towards 3.5% of GDP. The National Research Foundation (NRF), which reports directly to the prime minister, helps set the national innovation agenda and provides $5 billion in annual grants to companies to advance their individual R&D. The initial priority is not to create world-class tech utilities like Google and IBM, but to leverage their technologies to solve local problems and upgrade local capacity. Some call this strategy "second mover advantage." Singapore offers itself up as a "living lab" for foreign companies and universities to partner with government entities and universities (especially MIT and Switzerland's ETH-Zurich) to deploy driverless car test-beds, environmental sensor networks and data-security programs. Pharmaceutical companies have been drawn in to shiny new laboratories to conduct research and clinical trials across Asia. Meanwhile, the government rewards (with $10 million prizes) manufacturing companies that raise productivity in the face of regional competition, and reimburses start-up companies for technology-related costs such as computers, web design and app development.[12] At the One North complex near the National University of Singapore's campus, the buildings are named for the key functions essential to creating a productive ecosystem: Research, Innovation, Enterprise. Perhaps no such cluster will ever succeed the way Silicon Valley has, but by replicating some of its conditions, it can give the effort a big head start.

Warring for Talent

Info-states are highly strategic and selective about who gets in and why. Make no mistake: Switzerland and Singapore are already very diverse countries. Switzerland now has a close to 30 percent foreign-born population, the highest in Europe. But in 2014, the Swiss narrowly voted in favor of effectively overturning their 1999 agreement with the EU on the free movement of peoples, leveraging a "safeguard" clause in the treaty to mandate significant immigration restrictions. Singapore's population almost doubled between 1990 and 2010, with the foreign-born percentage of its population rising from 10 percent to almost 40 percent, making it second only to Dubai as a global melting pot. But in 2011, Singapore also began to severely restrict migration, responding to outcry over crowded public services and labor market preferences. Numerous job advertisements now declare "openings for Singaporeans only," and the "Singapore first" policy promotes locals in foreign firms.

---

12 Princeton economist Dani Rodrik argues that governments should go one step further and fund themselves from the investments made in profitable ventures and use the revenues to socialize the gains. This is precisely what Singapore now does, putting skin in the game by deploying its own capital in private venture funds through the Technology Incubation Scheme (TIS) and an Early Stage Venture Fund (ESVF).

This is what makes these info-states leaders in the global talent wars: Immigration policy strategically advances the aim of merit-based recruitment. With only three million citizens, Singapore has to compensate for labor shortages despite its world-class universities and polytechnics. It gives scholarships to foreigners followed by jobs in Singaporean companies and even government agencies. This in turn leads to granting permanent residency and a fast-track to citizenship. Foreigners thus become two-way ambassadors to their native lands, forging connections that their new home can take advantage of to boost commercial relationships. As foreigners come to outnumber locals, Singapore is learning to expand its permanent residency and citizenship population based on merit rather than racial quotas, becoming ever more a hub for global talent.

When I travel to countries such as Chile, the UAE, Kazakhstan, Rwanda, Georgia or a dozen other aspiring emerging markets, I am always presented with a sleek binder whose cover features some variation on "Vision" or "Strategy" for 2020, 2025 or 2030. All of them are about building world-class infrastructure, attracting value chains, building knowledge hubs, stimulating high-tech ecosystems and training talent for future skills. In other words, they are all copied and pasted from Singapore's master plan. After decades of importing intellectual capital, Singapore's model has become its own best export, raking in billions annually from contracts to build dozens of Singapore-style industrial parks across China, Vietnam, India, and now Africa and the Middle East, followed by corporate services to manage facilities and build local skills. In the reverse direction, delegations of Chinese, Indian and Kazakh officials, governors and mayors flock every few months to the Lee Kuan Yew School for executive training programs where they learn global best practices they can take home and implement tomorrow. The state-builders, urban planners, and economic strategists of the 21st century all take their inspiration from Lee Kuan Yew, not Thomas Jefferson.

Small States, Big Ideas

It could well be that the solution to every single major problem faced around the world today has a solution in small states rather than big ones. The idea that states as small as Singapore and Switzerland could be role models has been dismissed out of hand for decades. But today's world features growing numbers of effectively autonomous provinces and city-regions. As authority shifts from state to city, from federal to municipal, the comparison is no longer from state to state, but across these key decision-making units. In a world of city-states, it is the experience of large countries that has *less* relevance than ever. Success matters more than size.

In the most important measures of competitiveness, small states hold their weight and then some. There is an inverse correlation between the size of a country and the openness of its economy, with small states like Singapore, Switzerland, New Zealand, Finland and others topping the list. One-time Singaporean foreign minister Tommy Koh famously joked, "We would sign a free-trade agreement with the moon if we could." There is also a notable correlation between rankings in the Depth of Globalization Index and prosperity—and an inverse correlation to size—with top honors going to Hong Kong, Singapore, Luxembourg, Ireland and Belgium. By contrast, some of the world's most "shallow" countries in terms of global integration are large in size and population: Iran, Myanmar, Pakistan and

Bangladesh. The world has managed to ignore their populations despite their size, or until they emerge from tyranny or sanctions to make their assets accessible.

City-states are ground zero for finding solutions to the 21st century challenges of sustainable urbanization, managing diversity and navigating a turbulent global economy. The edge small states have is that they are already accustomed to strategizing for survival. They don't suffer from what America's Cold War grand strategist George Kennan called the "hubris of inordinate size." As the New Zealand scholar David Skilling points out, successful small states are strategically coherent and know their interests, focus relentlessly on their economic competitiveness, and adapt their focus as circumstances dictate.[13] With less inertia, they are more nimble, able to change policies more quickly. Fewer layers stand between decision-making leaders and the civil servants who implement policies, as they are often just down the hallway. There is a focused stack of federal, provincial and municipal authorities all functionally aligned with the same interests rather than competing with each other.

But being a small state isn't cheap. Delivering basic services such as schools and hospitals for a small population doesn't provide economies of scale. The up-front and maintenance costs for the military, railways, post offices, banks and other institutions and infrastructures are steep. With such small domestic markets, government support or co-investment is essential for

---

13 David Skilling, "In Praise of Small States," *Global Brief*, Spring/Summer 2013. Countries with small populations are the world's wealthiest in terms of per capita income: Norway, Qatar, Luxembourg, Macao, Switzerland, Denmark, Sweden, and Singapore. One sub-set of small states generally tops (in varying order) the rankings of economic freedom, competitiveness, attractiveness for foreign investment, social progress and effectiveness of public institutions: Hong Kong, Singapore, New Zealand, Switzerland, and Finland.

national utilities such as airlines or telecoms. Singapore is so small that there are no domestic flights; who would support its airline other than its own government? To this day the Swiss regret not propping up their national carrier Swiss Air rather than selling it to Germany's Lufthansa.

Small states are therefore very careful about costs and quality. Democracy doesn't teach the virtue of long-term saving as well as self-reliance does. Small countries that have precious raw materials (Norway) or financial surpluses (Singapore) have been wiser about saving them in sovereign wealth funds that make strategic developmental investments or help maintain financial stability during downturns. It is also the smaller sub-state territories such as Alaska and Western Australia that have such funds, while larger countries such as England and Canada have neglected to create them despite their resource riches. Building strategic petroleum reserves when oil is cheap, or setting up sovereign wealth funds to ensure the solvency of pensions, are the actions of technocratic thinking pioneered by small states.

Small states, or cities and provinces, merge technocratic ideas with democratic practice far better than large state, experimenting much more proactively within their administrative boundaries rather than wait for approval from far-off capitals. While Canada's greenhouse gas emissions have skyrocketed due to tar sands oil production, Quebec has launched a carbon exchange (with California) and an electric transportation initiative. It also has far stronger rules for gun registrations. Similarly, Scotland raised taxes on alcohol higher than the rest of the UK to curb unruly behavior. Even though such interventions have occurred in democratic societies to promote environmental sustainability and public welfare, they are highly technocratic in how they were conceived and managed.

Edwark Luttwak, a noted scholar of imperial grand strategy, has often remarked that America's defense and intelligence agencies would be far more effective if their budgets were cut in half. In other words, if they were forced to operate like lean and focused small states. At a time when Western governments are bloated and ineffective, small states strive to be lean and efficient, carefully monitoring their finances and pensions. The Dutch, for example, save assiduously, deploy sizeable annuities for retirees, and are shifting the next generation labor force towards an on-demand structure while taxing companies more to pay for the added costs of portable insurance. At the same time, the gross impunities of large countries aren't possible in small open countries where the public scrutinizes the government closely. The world's least corrupt countries according to Transparency International are all small states: Denmark, New Zealand, Finland, Sweden, Singapore, Switzerland and the Netherlands.

If all states acted like small states, they would have no choice but to focus on human capital since they could not rely on hinterlands or natural resources. Indeed, small states also emphasize education more than large ones. The top scorers in the PISA education rankings are Finland and Estonia. "Singapore Math" is a global export. Making each person count helps small states become innovators and disruptors. Two Estonian start-ups, Skype and TransferWise, are disrupting the entire arenas of telecommunications and financial transfers.

Widespread connectivity is of course a precondition for a successful 21st century society society. Places that provide ubiquitous high-speed Internet and convenient digital services for business rank high in the WEF's Network Readiness Index. Again, small states such as Sweden, Finland, Singapore and

Switzerland top the list. They also have the lowest taxes and tariffs on the import or purchase and consumption of ICT services precisely because they are proven to make economies more efficient and individuals more productive.[14] By providing universal digital services, they make it possible for entrepreneurs to save immensely on start-up costs for business. Not surprisingly, small states are also among the strongest advocates of an open Internet.

Despite perceptions that Scandinavian societies are coddled welfare states, Sweden has managed to forge a path of flexible labor markets coupled with mandated wage hikes of about 2% per year. Swedes flip that consumption power into productivity and digitization plans such as shifting towards a cashless society. Sweden already has a disproportionate number of leading global companies from IKEA and Ericsson to Volvo and H&M, with major companies ploughing dividends back into research to give rise to the next wave of growth companies. Sweden's shrewd state-funded innovation agency Vinnova incubates the successors to the country's wildly popular streaming music service Spotify.

Sweden's neighbor Finland is another democracy that excels at strategic planning. It has a parliamentary committee devoted to analyzing likely future parameters for policy-making (based on either global policy regulations or resource constraints) and devising ways for policy-makers to preemptively adapt to them. The Netherlands has run a multi-year exercise plotting scenarios for the world in 2030 and developing economic strategies accordingly. Agencies and bodies such as these—cutting across the

---

14 Ben Miller and Robert D. Atkinson, *Digital Drag: Ranking 125 Nations by Taxes and Tariffs on ICT Goods and Services, Information Technology and Innovation Foundation*, October 2014.

branches of government—can openly deliberate controversial yet ultimately technical measures such as setting aside 1% or more of annual federal budgets for future investments. Precisely because their mandate is to confront complexity head-on, they can think and act in apolitical ways even though they are political bodies.

Big countries can learn too. Deng Xiaoping famously launched China's economic reforms and established Shenzhen as the country's first SEZ after a visit to Singapore. His aim was not to build a giant Singapore, but rather to replicate Singapore as many times as possible within China. Since that time, Singaporean authorities have designed, built and managed industrial parks, technology zones and eco-districts in Suzhou, Tianjin, Guangzhou, Chongqing, Wuxi, Jilin, and several other cities and provinces.

Amongst large Western democracies, Germany comes closest to being an info-state. The federal government takes a lead role in areas where up-front investment creates platform infrastructure with nation-wide benefits such as the "Digitales Deutschland" initiative to achieve one hundred percent broadband connectivity. It has also merged its economic and energy ministries, making investments in clean energy that promote national security, create new industries such as renewable power, and raise productivity all at the same time. A situation such as America's massively wasteful healthcare spending—it costs four times as much per capita as Germany's but with pitiful results—is intolerable in master-planned Germany. Because Germany provides the national infrastructural foundations for each province's cities and industries to be connected to global markets, each region has a viable business plan for itself. Most of the world's best cars come from Germany—but from three different provinces constantly seeking to out-do each other in performance.

For this reason, there is no country that is admired more in China today than Germany, and no foreign leader who visits China more or has more influence there than Angela Merkel (who tops the list of foreign leaders most admired in America as well). China has little to learn from Washington and everything to learn from Frankfurt and Berlin: Well-regulated companies with capital and labor sharing in management, inclusive and pro-social politics, and high value-added innovation making an export powerhouse. China, the most populous empire in history, is trying to reorganize itself into a collection of two dozen urban technocratic hubs. America should do the same.

3.
SEVEN PRESIDENTS ARE BETTER THAN ONE

From Oval Office to Round Table

What the world's oldest democracy (Switzerland), shiniest city-state technocracy (Singapore), and newest superpower (China) all have in common is that while they nominally have only one "head of state," each is in fact a *collective presidency,* led by a committee of seven whose complementary portfolios bring them together in a joint management structure. Their cabinet members don't act as individuals in bureaucratic silos, but as a team since they are all accountable for the success of the whole system.

Now more than ever, America too needs more presidents. Having just elected the first president with no government experience whatsoever, the US needs a corporate board like structure steering the nation rather than just one man. At the same time, the world has become so complex that no one person can juggle so many balls in the air at the same time. Seven heads are better than one, period.

Even in the world's oldest democracy, the people don't directly elect their president. Swiss citizens vote for the parliament, which then appoints the seven-member Federal Executive Council.

While Switzerland has almost twenty political parties, the Council includes at least one member from each of the four main parties whose coalition has dominated for over fifty years. Building opposition permanently into the Council (a practice known as concordance) guarantees that all perspectives are considered but without leading to stasis. The Swiss balance has been dubbed the "magic formula," and indeed what is most striking is how the system is completely democratic—yet totally technocratic—at the same time. A process that ensures policy continuity among a cross-section of leaders across multiple parties is far superior to political systems that simply flip-flop among two parties in predictable cycles of voter fatigue. This is how to construct a "team of rivals."

Since Lee Kuan Yew's passing from the political scene nearly two decades ago, Singapore has begun to move in the Swiss direction. Despite being Lee Kuan Yew's son, prime minister Lee Hsien Loong doesn't rule by fiat. There are two deputy prime ministers who divide administrative oversight roughly between security and home affairs and economic and social policy, and a dozen other cabinet ministers, each of whom has done rotations across other ministries. Every two years, party members elect 12-18 members of a Central Executive Committee (CEC) that helps steer the leadership agenda. Lee himself was a deputy prime minister for 14 years, so hardly a political novice. Soon even Singapore's once ceremonial president will be directly elected by the people, codifying new authorities such as safeguarding the country's vast financial reserves against any outlandish populist spending proposals.

When a fairly young cabinet member in Singapore was made foreign minister in 2015, I asked a friend who would be his mentor. After all, in the US, a new secretary of state or presidential candidate needs to be seen having lunch with Henry Kissinger for us to feel that he or she knows how to find Russia on a map. But in Singapore, the most recent foreign minister is still sitting in the cabinet, with the three before him always on call to provide insight. They don't draw on greybeards but work in real-time with those who handled the portfolio immediately before them.

The seven members of China's Politburo Standing Committee (PSC) are also elected based on their merit and experience. Each member serves tours in multiple provinces (some of which may have populations as large as America) covering portfolios ranging from industry to agriculture to education. They may not have experience in representative democracy, but they actually know how to govern and are judged on their performance: The 2013 National People's Congress (NPC) gathered 3000 delegates who ranked the selection of premier Li Keqiang's cabinet. Most of the 25 ministers selected had satisfaction ratings of over 98%, but those chosen for education, environment, housing and rural development had only 93% approval—and received vocal jeers from delegates. Expectations are highest on the issues that count the most.

Zhang Weiwei, a scholar at Fudan University who was the former interpreter for Deng Xiaoping, calls the Chinese model a mix of selection and election. There are no doubt rivalries in the PSC: Xi Jinping is as mercurial as Chinese leaders come, and he has shifted influence in economic affairs from premier Li to his own special advisory committees. Having won the designation as the "core" leader of the Party, some suggest Xi will even dump Li at the halfway mark in 2017. But the PSC itself is a team—and one that has a full decade to execute policies before passing the baton. Whomever Xi chooses as his successor will have at least a half decade of full participation in governing China before becoming first among equals.

Despite running the world's largest country, Chinese leaders don't seem to complain about being overwhelmed, distracted or exhausted. One reason is that they have graduated from rule by decree to rule by committee. Remember that communist China and capitalist China were both built by the same Party. The era of central planning lasted from 1949-1979, while since then the government has gained almost four decades' experience with markets. The many self-corrections China's leadership has undertaken paint a different picture from Western clichés of the Party being rigid and illegitimate, whereas in fact it is remarkably adaptive. China's ability to get so much done during each generation's tenure is often written off as the obvious consequence of being a single-party state. But it has as much to do with its collective leadership structure. The seven-member Central Standing Committee is backed by a 25-member politburo and a Central Committee of 350 members who appoint most key Party and Military figures and debate all aspects of policy. The collective approach involves all top leaders in matters of regional affairs, the economy, legislation, anti-corruption and national security, meaning each Standing Committee member is far more involved in national governance than an American cabinet secretary who is only responsible for one portfolio. Collective leadership can also be a great asset in foreign policy. Xi Jinpeng and Li Keqiang traveled to a combined 50 countries in their first two years at the helm of the Party, signing hundreds of billions of dollars of trade and investment agreements while also pursuing an ambitious domestic reform agenda. Xi may be dogmatic in the pursuit of national stability, but he is not a "bad emperor" that will plunge China into a megalomaniacal abyss.

In China and Singapore, it would be unheard of for anyone to ascend to national leadership without having first acquired and practiced significant executive administration of a territory or state bureaucracy. According to Lee Kuan Yew, a good president should be someone who has been either a long-serving minister or a CEO of a publicly traded company, someone who understands how to herd cats to produce a workable budget. His ideal leader was a math geeks with leadership skills and imagination. Just as bankers should be less flashy, so too should politicians. Today's leaders need to be more than just debaters; they should be multi-functional administrators.

Only one American president, Franklin D. Roosevelt, has led the country for more than a decade, the timeframe so many agree is necessary to enact and see through major policy changes. In a tenure spanning the Great Depression through World War II, Roosevelt, through his New Deal policies, initiated massive employment generating schemes such as the Tennessee Valley Authority and the Works Progress Administration and created Social Security, the Securities and Exchange Commission (SEC) and the Federal Deposit Insurance Corporation (FDIC), putting the economy back on its feet and institutionalizing safeguards against future financial crises. By contrast, Obama's eight years in the White House have been a continuous exercise in damage control from the financial crisis and the wars in Iraq and Afghanistan, interrupted by his own reelection campaign and mid-term Congressional elections in which the Democrats lost ground. In America, there is a clear trade-off between action and elections, between policy and politics.

President Obama and his predecessors in the Oval Office have also been known to remark how glad they are to not have to run for re-election once into their second term so that they can finally focus on policy. But should focusing on policy rather being distracted by politics really have to wait four years? Would it not be better for the president to serve just one single term of six or eight years, as numerous experts have recommended?

The famous remark by current European Commission president Jean-Claude Juncker during his nearly two-decade long tenure as Luxembourg's prime minister—"We all know what to do, but don't know how to get re-elected once we've done it"—begs the question: Is it more important to do what needs to be done or to get reelected? The EU is accused of have a "democracy deficit," but in fact it needs to give its technocrats more leeway to actually implement policies that build Europe rather than caving in to populists who would dismantle it.

In his first term, Obama constructed a "team of rivals," but abandoned the egotistical cacophony in his second term in favor of a loyal echo chamber. Obama's centralizing approach may have been unintentional, but it repeats a pattern of past presidents that reveals a deep disjunction between the ideal and reality of America's executive leadership: The American president winds up acting like an imperious executive, but without acknowledging it. It does not help that America's cabinet members serve at the pleasure of the president—but also to the extent that it pleases them until they rush off after a few years to Wall Street, memoir writing and the speaker's circuit. It is difficult to know who is serving in the public interest if government service is a personal privilege rather than a professional vocation.

By contrast, in parliamentary systems such as in Britain and its former colony Singapore, the cabinet is comprised entirely of elected members of parliament, and committee processes select the most qualified to rise into the cabinet. These systems are therefore *more* democratic (and also more meritocratic) than America's cabinet, to which any friend of the president can be appointed. Rarely does one have the kind of amateur hour that has been witnessed in Obama's cabinet with underwhelming secretaries handling key portfolios such as labor, education and transportation. (No doubt this will be prove to be the case as well under Trump.) Furthermore, with the inherently siloed nature of today's cabinet, the president is virtually alone in "connecting the dots" despite the growing complexity of challenges, with little high-level support to consider scenarios and calculate trade-offs.

America could take a big step towards a smarter executive branch if the cabinet were a true collective presidency with more consultative decision-making and fewer silos of authority. Since there is no mention of the cabinet in the constitution, the president can construct it any way he chooses. In fact, he should include senior members of Congress elected by their peers, as well as selected governors with deep experience (see below). Congressmen are not prohibited from advising the president by serving as auxiliary or rotating cabinet members, much as they might accept a committee appointment. Such a cabinet would be doubly democratic since it would contain not only an elected president but also elected legislators. Furthermore, it would be a legitimate "team of rivals" with far more bipartisan credibility as well as greater leverage over Congress itself than the president does. Importantly, the cabinet in a such a collective presidency would be made of individuals who have real skin in the game, deeply vested in results and outcomes rather than brinksmanship.

To be more effective, the number of cabinet portfolios should also be reduced to create functional coordination rather than wasteful duplication of activities and agencies working at cross purposes. Some obvious examples: The Department of Transportation and Department of Housing and Urban Development could be combined into an Infrastructure Department; the departments of Energy, Agriculture and Interior, as well as the Environmental Protection Agency (EPA), should be fused into a Department of Energy and Environment; the Department of Commerce with the US Trade Representative; Defense with Homeland Security; Education with Labor; and so on (see chart). Irrespective of the Cabinet's size, an Executive Committee within the Cabinet would be the central decision-making body, comprised of the President, Vice President, and 5-7 other key portfolios such as defense, treasury, justice and infrastructure. In all, about half the cabinet would be made up of individuals who have been directly elected to their simultaneous positions, a quarter made up of experienced civil servants, and a quarter personally invited by the president.

Indeed, to introduce disruptive change into government thinking, there is nothing wrong with talented corporate and civic leaders joining the cabinet for four-year positions. For example, if the US actually wanted to rapidly move towards a national broadband network, there would be few better to lead the charge than John Chambers of IT giant Cisco, who knows both internet infrastructure and how to run a corporate behemoth. Already the White House's Jobs and Competitiveness Council is stacked with CEOs and executives such as GE's Jeff Immelt and Facebook's Sheryl Sandberg, as is the Department of Defense's Advisory Board. But rather than having these ad hoc and fleeting gatherings with no real authority, the government needs statutory inter-agency bodies that make real policy.

Having a technocratically empowered cabinet is particularly important to overcome the nearly perpetual reality of divided government. The White House and Congress have only been controlled by the same party for 26 years since 1945. Unable to gain Congressional cooperation to pass legislation, the past four presidents have issued in total nearly one thousand executive orders, with Obama alone accounting for more than half. In matters such as healthcare, food safety, worker protection, air pollution, the minimum wage, airline passenger rights, net neutrality and drones, the Obama administration used legal levers to reshape regulations rather than pursue futile dealings with Congress until time ran out. But recent years have witnessed significant Congressional challenge to the president's executive authority on immigration, war and spending. What began as political maneuverings threaten to become Constitutional crises unless authorities are clarified rather than left opaque.

Now that the Republicans control the White House, Congress and Supreme Court, only a collective presidency approach featuring a diversity of views can both compensate for Trump's lack of experience and check his potential demagogical whims. Rather than shooting from the hip, he would have to spend all day with and win over a half-dozen other senior executive figures (almost all of whom would be more experienced in government than himself). And given Trump's age—similar to Ronald Reagan's at inauguration—a collectively presidency could better manage the scheduling rigors of domestic political consultations and international diplomatic forays than any single leader. Is that not a superior model than one man making ultimate decisions alone, backed by a vice president whose role most people don't even understand?

The Best and the Brightest

It is just as important for the effectiveness of the executive branch that the president and cabinet be supported by a strong civil service that maintains the proper functioning of government agencies. A professional civil service is crucial to maintaining a gap between party and state, for its members are stewards of national governance who know how to administer the state, not a cadre of self-interested political cronies. Simply put: A civil service gets things done even if elected politicians do nothing.

In the UK, the civil service designs the entire federal budget and submits it to parliament for feedback and approval before it is executed. And yet it's hard to imagine a technocratic system ever plunging itself headlong into a political vacuum such as the "Brexit." By some accounts, stormy weather kept many complacent "Remain" voters at home, allowing the "Leave" camp to narrowly prevail. Does a smart country consign itself to strategic oblivion based on a simple majority vote on a rainy day? After the Brexit results emerged, a civil service committee was hastily cobbled together to examine the implications of the decision. In a proper technocracy, the civil service studies the scenarios and consequences of issues *before* the parliament or people decide which course to take—not after. Then, parliament could consult actively with the citizenry before taking a vote requiring a two-thirds super-majority.

The still-unfolding Brexit debacle underscores that the triumph of politics over rationality is almost as acute in Britain as in the US. And it is no surprise: Since 1973, the UK's civil service has been slashed by more than one-third to under 450,000 staff. A decade ago, journalist Anthony Sampson provocatively wrote *Who*

Runs this Place?, an acerbic analysis of British politics concluding that the combination of recycled politicians, shady special interests and a neutered civil service meant that democracy had been stripped of both accountability and effectiveness. Everyone is feeding at the trough; nobody is manning the wheel.

Today it is Singapore's civil service that ranks highest in the world both in terms of its capacity and bureaucratic autonomy. All cabinet ministers are matched to permanent secretaries from the civil service who know the beat inside out. Singapore's civil service is a spiral staircase: With each rung you learn to manage a different portfolio, building a broad knowledge base and first-hand experience. By contrast, American politics is like an elevator: One can get in on the bottom floor and go straight to top, missing all the learning in between.

American strategists revere Andy Marshall, the recently retired director of the DoD's Office of Net Assessment (ONA) that creates war scenarios and futuristic battle concepts to confront them. Singaporean Siong Guan Lim—who, like Andy Marshall, is nicknamed "Yoda"—is a mechanical engineer who served as permanent secretary for defense, education and finance, ran the Economic Development Board (EDB), Civil Service and Prime Minister's Office, and chaired the Government Investment Corporation (GIC) sovereign wealth fund. He is known for rarely imposing an idea but always seeking to generate a collective vision among colleagues. The same is true of Peter Ho of the Center for Strategic Futures (CSF), the government's internal think-tank. What they have in common is broad experience across many government departments, the authority to conduct independent research, and their advocacy of "whole of society" policies across bureaucratic divides. Either of them—and the many hundreds of civil servant technocrats they have trained and inspired—have the toolkit to run a country of any size.

The current head of Singapore's civil service, , has initiated a process of broadening all bureaucrats' training to cope with complexity. The civil service now recruits for deeper expertise in economic strategy, infrastructure planning, environmental stewardship, security and defense, social services and bureaucratic administration. Urban planning, for example, is handled by teams meshing architects, economists, demographers, ecologists and many other experts. Rather than build more vertical bureaucracies, such horizontal mechanisms pool resources and apply them to functional challenges such as monitoring borders and aviation, tracking supply chains, ensuring food security, and protecting critical infrastructure. Along the way, generalists become specialists and vice-versa, and the cross-pollination leads to innovative problem-solving. Because policy is as serious as any war, Singapore's Civil Service College (CSC) has invested more than $10 million in simulations that resemble Pentagon war-gaming, focusing on disruptive technologies and energy supplies and generally imagining "black swans."

By moving bureaucrats around yet also nurturing expertise, Singapore prevents civil servants from becoming "dead wood" as they do in America's federal agencies. And by cultivating professionals rather than outsourcing to over-paid contractors, knowledge is collected, internalized and adapted. Info-states leverage the case studies, stress tests and systems integration of enterprise applications that consultants offer, but make sure their civil servants absorb the know-how to take on such strategic projects themselves, becoming the rightful stewards of useful data. Singapore is the toughest assignment for management consultants: They never get to offer the same service twice.

Good governance often comes down to a combination of statistics and logistics: Analyzing data and getting things done. Other countries have engineers in politics; America has barely a handful. One explanation offered by science historian Edward Tenner is that distrust of government and a strong private sector have lured engineers away from government. Yet government needs more engineers—fixers and plumbers—rather than financiers. Singapore's civil service attracts mathematics, engineering and technology talent while Washington scares it away. Google's Hal Varian once claimed that statistician is the sexiest career of the 21st century. In Singapore, at least, he is correct.

China and Singapore's civil service ranks are full of boring perfectionists, but what they lack in charisma they make up for in creativity. Singapore's CSC and China's CELAP have become the epicenters of thinking about composite government models that mix democracy and data. It is in these organizations that the field of public administration has evolved into a "policy science" that leverages global case studies to adapt institutions to generate better outcomes. Not dissimilar to the ancient Confucian emphasis on justly rule by princes, today's Chinese Communist Party requires anywhere from one month to one year of training at the Central Party School every five years, while the leadership goes on annual retreats to different provinces to study progress and challenges in the countryside. By contrast, America's more than two million federal civil servants (including half a million postal service workers) across more than 400 agencies have little incentive, and certainly no mandate, to learn from other countries.

Max Weber, the father of modern government science, would be gravely worried by the declining independence and professionalism of American government bureaucracies. Institutional memory—the accumulation of historical knowledge—fades as professionals retire and short-term politicians consult neither the repository of experience nor the experts who have lived through it. To reverse this decay, America's federal service needs to have an existence and ethos outside of the rank and file of each cabinet department. America has many fine bureaucrats, but they do not add up to the entrepreneurial bureaucracy that a modern civil service should be, one that has the resources to think long-term and the mandate to be impartial and independent of political directives. That is why there should be a sizeable permanent staff with a statutory budget that brings all departments up to speed.

Within the White House, crucial advisory bodies such as the National Security Council (NSC) and Council of Economic Advisors (CEA) should have more statutory and policy-making authority than their currently vague mandates allow. Congressional committees and other government agencies could provide inputs to these bodies but not overrule them. The paradox of the NSC and CEA today is that they have the most pedigreed members but an inadequate number of permanent positions. As a result, talented advisors cycle through but depart quickly to avoid the lengthy lame duck election periods, leaving a vacuum in management of key portfolios. Rather than being run by appointees from outside, these bodies should be run by top-tier experts with appointees rotating in with fresh outside thinking. With a stronger permanent staff, the NSC could do a better job of quarterbacking inter-agency strategic planning, improving on today's still pathetically uncoordinated agendas of the DoD, CIA and State Department.

The Office of Science and Technology Policy (OSTP) is another example of a technical group staffed with experts who are up to speed on the latest developments in everything from alternative energy to nano-materials to neuroscience. They should have far more latitude to designate crucial research centers such as the National Additive Manufacturing Innovation Institute (NAMII) located in Ohio. In a good technocracy, cable companies, telecoms and IT firms would not squabble endlessly over "net neutrality" before broadband gets designated as a utility (which finally happened in 2014 with a ruling favoring the FCC's position). There is a difference between heavy-handed regulation and incentivizing progressive shifts in business practices, a nuance navigated by the White House Office of Information and Regulatory Affairs (OIRA), whose technocrats such as Harvard Law School professor Cass Sunstein consult with experts and citizens to model outcomes and generate a spectrum of policy choices.

It may seem odd to advocate strengthening executive authority after an election that has brought a political neophyte into the White House. But this is about building and institutionalizing technocratic competence *beyond* the president—especially so as to limit the damage any one president can do. Washington needs more such civil servants who, in the words of journalist James Traub, "believe in reason, expertise and the lessons of history." Those are the virtues of genuine technocracy, not American democracy. The American public is rightly fed up with the country's political aristocracy—but don't confuse Martha's Vineyard millionaires and the political hacks who serve them for dedicated civil servants. The present Beltway elite is largely a self-referential scrum of opportunistic amateurs, not a rigorously qualified and far-sighted technocracy.

The Meritocracy Behind Technocracy

Democracy guarantees neither that good ideas emerge nor that they get implemented. Finding and executing on the best ideas is far more likely in a meritocratic system, which is why meritocracy is the lifeblood of the true technocracy. It is the back-end talent management system that ensures a steady supply of experts trained in the critical social and technical sciences to manage state affairs. A meritocracy is not just about intellectual achievements but tangible experience. It promotes good people from within rather than circumventing them with political appointees. Lee Kuan Yew always stressed the importance of an effective and non-corrupt administrative bureaucracy that enforced the rule of law. Singapore's annual audit of all public and publicly financed institutions is a transparent naming and shaming exercise, putting online and on the front pages of the *Straits Times* any lapses in fiduciary or other standards from banks to universities. Just one percentage point lower than expected returns on on the sovereign wealth fund GIC's portfolio or the CPF pension pool and citizens start to howl.

Designing government to minimize corruption involves crucial modifications. One well-known cure for corruption Singapore leads the way in is having highly paid ministers whose visibility essentially demands that they view government service as a trusteeship rather than a pathway to later wealth. Even after slashing the salaries of cabinet ministers and other senior officials by one-third to one-half in 2012, they are still the highest paid public servants in the world. (Civil servants also get very modest bonuses tied to national economic performance.) High salaries allow Singapore's political class to become landowners and thus have a disproportionate stake in the property market, but they have also acted against self-interest by dramatically forcing down prices in recent years in response to public pressure.

Always beware the oligarch in disguise. In Turkey and Russia, strongmen declare themselves to be technocrats while running elaborate mafia regimes. These are mafia states, not technocracies. Real technocrats are not Gucci-wearing thugs, nor Islamist wolves in sheep's clothing. They aren't in such a hurry to get rich quick, offshore their capital, or hoard executive powers. In Singapore, they often just wear short-sleeve Batik shirts and flip-flops and attend book talks. Newer approaches to measuring the efficacy of public administration veer ever more in the meritocratic direction. For example, a 2013 report published by Germany's Hertie School of Governance emphasizes impartial hiring and promotion, the statistical capacity for collection and diagnosis of social and economic data, and the intellectual resources of government as measured by the number of advanced degree holders employed.[15]

Meritocracy mitigates revolutionary demands because—unlike monarchy, aristocracy, or dictatorship—there is a sense that higher social standing and leadership are open to all based on their skills and hard work. But meritocracy finds little fertile soil in a climate where rhetoric has replaced logic and everyone is entitled to their own facts. Churchill famously quipped that "the best argument against democracy is a five-minute conversation with the average voter." How about with the average presidential candidate? The 2016 election featured no less than a dozen candidates who could easily have been dis-allowed from running in the first place through a simple intellectual background check.

---

15   Hertie School of Governance, *Governance Report 2013*. Oxford University Press.

As Frank Bruni commented in the *New York Times,* candidates such as Scott Walker treated the presidential campaign as a series of pop quizzes for which one watches Sunday talk shows to prepare, while Ben Carson gave his own new interpretation of the Constitution each week. Their brand of post-truth politics only validates the anti-political cynicism of the public.

American-style political oligarchy is neither technocracy nor meritocracy. In a meritocracy, declaring a candidate "unfit" or "unqualified" is not merely a campaign epithet but a measurable proposition. Trump won the election even though most voters felt he was unqualified to be president. In America, "electability" clearly refers to being capable of winning an election, whereas in a meritocracy it would mean one's deservedness to do so. Furthermore, saying things that are unconstitutional and unethical doesn't just make you figuratively disqualified, but literally disqualified. In racing to find out what will happen next, we have lost all sight of what should or should not happen at all.

Even a meritocratic technocracy like Singapore does need to be careful not to slip into rent-seeking oligarchy. In recent years, Singapore's government has risked a rupture from a substantial swath of the people because of the education funnel that feeds the upper echelon of politics and commerce is populated with the privileged class, leading many to perceive that the ladder is only lowered periodically for people from less elite rungs. Long-standing PAP parliamentarians—including an education minister and foreign minister—have been tossed out in elections for appearing elitist during campaigns (for example, by showing up in fancy cars though most people don't own one). Some people simply want to see unexpected faces with unconventional backgrounds appear in the country's top ranks. Either way, technocrats must be sure to get out of their air-conditioned offices as often as possible and not confuse being busy brainstorming with being efficacious in governing.

Chinese leaders have also come to fear the backlash against perceived indifference to extreme inequality that reflects a gap between the Party and the people. Indeed, prominent princelings and Party elites have colluded with land developers and state-owned industries to amass fortunes: The Party is allegedly the world's largest club of billionaires. From 1990-2010, an estimated 18,000 party members have fled China with as much as $120 billion. Nonetheless, for the time being the Party remains respected and trusted in China due to the tangible improvements in quality of life it has delivered.

Though no system is perfect, the premium on having a meritocratic executive branch and civil service requires structural innovation. In *The China Model*, Canadian political theorist Daniel Bell rightly points to how meritocracy, experimentation and decisiveness have catapulted Chinese modernization in ways democracy might well have hindered. He advocates a further evolution towards a "vertical democratic meritocracy": Democracy at the bottom (since municipal leaders are actually popular and can respond to rapid feedback), experimentation in the middle (such as provinces attracting investment and supporting industries that suit their natural resources and human capital), and meritocracy at the top (so that there can be consistent long-term policy implementation). This is arguably the right model not just for China but any sensible country.

The Technocratic Mantra: Utilitarianism

Technocrats are known to be good at weighing means and ends, costs and benefits, causes and effects. But to avoid veering into elitist indifference, technocrats must think with the head and the heart at the same time. They cannot be Soviet-era central planners for whom citizens were cogs in defunct ideological wheels. Rather, they must blend democracy and data, foresight and feeling. Max Weber believed that ethical professionals view the public trust and welfare as a core responsibility. They have a higher calling to improve society, not just temporarily lead it. In this spirit, technocratic leaders should be what Bell calls a "compassionate meritocracy" in which officials are rewarded for demonstrating corruption-free behavior and actions taken in the public interest.

The creed of a good technocracy must therefore be utilitarianism, allocating resources to achieve large-scale social mobility and benefit. Its objective is not only wealth maximization but also welfare maximization—a mix of Adam Smith and Jeremy Bentham—both the flourishing (and protection) of individual liberty as well as the promotion of fair and equal opportunity and benefit. In this way utilitarianism is a crucial bridge between democratic ideals and democracy in practice. While democratic leaders merely look at polls, technocratic leaders should look at people.

Europe's austerity policies in response to the financial crisis have been painful examples of non-utilitarian thinking by national leaders and financial regulators. Extreme spending cuts were been both inhumane and counter-productive: Tightening the belt on the poor only served to contract the economy and increase insecurity. Austerity does not create jobs, raise incomes, generate taxes or boost consumption.

America too has suffered from a deficit of utilitarian thinking. The Wall Street bail-out engineered by then Federal Reserve chairman Ben Bernanke and Treasury secretary Tim Geithner is credited with saving the financial system, but no correspondingly robust and unconventional policy was engineered for Main Street such as "helicopter drops" of cash to the poorest 80 percent of Americans. Massachusetts senator Elizabeth Warren, whose advocacy led to the creation of the US Consumer Financial Protection Bureau (CFPB), supports such approaches that give more direct financial support to the American middle class. A century ago, the Gilded Age gave way to the Progressive Era through far-reaching interventions such as housing settlements for the underclass and curbing corruption in federal agencies and Congress. Only utilitarian thinking can bring about another progressive era.

There need not be a tension between democratic means and utilitarian ends—technocrats have to heed the former and deliver the latter. Along the way, they cannot be uncompromising automatons. They must regularly hold up the mirror and see the data reflected back in the form of results and public satisfaction. Citizens armed with real-time information want a voice in policy—but also want experts providing viable policy options. An informed public may respect and trust its leaders for their competence, but it will judge them by their performance, not their credentials.

4.
PARLIAMENTS FOR THE PEOPLE

Politics Without Policy

With an effective collective presidency and robust technocratic civil service, the executive branch of an info-state is a formidable organ of power. Plato's Guardians are firmly in the driver's seat. But legislatures need to modernize as well, both to serve as a check on executive power, as well as to better fulfill their own responsibilities to represent citizens' interests.

Unfortunately, America has degenerated into politics without democracy when it should aspire to democracy without politics. Politics is no longer the ideal of persuasion but the narrow horse-trading among special interests, while democracy is no longer the voice of the citizens but rule by a political class that preserves the status quo. Americans get elections without action, or action that does not match their preferences. Harvard lecturer Yascha Mounk calls this system "undemocratic liberalism," meaning rights are protected but institutions don't translate popular will into public policy. As Princeton scholar Martin Gilens and Benjamin Page of Northwestern pointed out in their widely cited research, when the preferences of average voters diverge from those of the elite, Congress votes for the elite without exception.[16] Their conclusion: America is an oligarchy—governed by a corrupt, rent-seeking elite—not a democracy.

Legal scholars such as Harvard's Lawrence Lessig argue that the process of representative democracy in America is equivalent to institutionalized corruption. Indeed, there is nothing meritocratic about a two-stage electoral system in which there is a "money election" driven by super-PACs funders to determine which candidates are approved to appear in general elections. While there is no mention of political parties in the Constitution, they at least created an informal procedural code and policy discipline. Today, rather than being driven by members they are manipulated by donors who dictate the slate of candidates and shape the party's agenda. Thanks to the Citizens United ruling, corporations have become "persons," but unlike humans who vote only every several years, companies get to exercise their financial "speech" on a daily basis and at ever-greater volume. The resulting PAC-directed political parties constitute not a meritocracy but what Lessig calls a "fund-ocracy."

Congressmen spend so little time actually making laws that they have failed to pass all their spending bills on time for two decades. About half of America's Congressmen and Senators became millionaires in business before running for office, and while in Congress they are equal parts lobbyist and lawmaker but spend most of their time preparing for re-election. Upon retirement they return to full-time lobbying. Given this reality, how likely is radical change from within such as campaign finance reform, scrapping primaries, reforming (or abolishing)

---

16 Gilens and Page, "Testing Theories of American Politics: Elites, Interest Groups, and Average Citizens," *Perspectives on Politics* (2014).

the antiquated electoral college, or imposing term limits?

Perhaps Congress should be thought of not as an independent branch of government but rather the agent of a more powerful force. In his recent book *Deep State*, veteran Congressional analyst Mike Lofgren argues that the covert nexus of military and financial professionals operating inside the Beltway has become "the most complex institution the world has ever known," manipulating lawmakers while even superseding them in access and influence. Having pilfered from the system and paid off Congress to tax-exempt its profits, this deep state may soon have little use for Congress itself anymore. But corruption is a two-way street. Congress knows well how to extort business to stay in business: The number of temporary tax credits has skyrocketed, with Congressmen shaking down corporate donors to fill their coffers before renewing the credits at the 11th hour.

Indirect democracy has also become an invitation for gerrymandering districts to create safe seats from which Tea Party radicals can hijack the House, while the Senate's structure allows a minority of rural voters to outmaneuver the majority. While James Madison feared the tyranny of the majority, the new threat has become the tyranny of the minority. In 2013, Congressional Republicans effectively shut down the government in an effort to repeal spending provisions for just one bill, the Affordable Care Act. As democracy observer Ivan Krastev has noted, American democracy is a game of chicken in which preventing the other side from governing is more important than governing yourself.

The chaos of democracy may be beautiful, but it's not worth the price of making a country ungovernable. America's political system is now unable to escape itself, to design laws that anticipate their own unintended consequences and make society better. The many overlapping and conflicting layers, mandates and budgets across the federal, state and municipal level in healthcare, education, infrastructure and other areas creates opacity and confusion, while special interests, lawyers and consultants exploit the chaos.[17] As it stands today, Congressional politics not only fails to bring forth good ideas but results in laws that resemble either Swiss cheese for all their loopholes or the bird-reptile-mammal Platypus for their bizarre complexity. For example, Obamacare has been so saddled with technical difficulties and inconsistent claims that many describe it as a "partial circumcision." Insurance companies have been liberated to game their policies while would-be doctors see less incentive in taking up the medical profession. Similarly, Dodd-Frank was so over-burdened with regulatory guidelines that it is keeping American companies from investing domestically at a time when it is needed most, or pushing them abroad to less-regulated markets from which they can operate more efficiently.

Transparency in Congressional affairs has simultaneously lowered trust in government, encouraged presidents to govern by executive order, and provoked long-term devolutionary efforts by states and cities to avoid the corruption and delays of federal politics altogether. But because Congressional approval is essential for large-scale spending on infrastructure, the military and other national services, we must worry that without restoring trust in the legislature, crucial initiatives will be neglected to the detriment of society as a whole.

Those who don't understand the mechanisms of power in

---

17   Steven Teles, "Klugeocracy in America," *National Affairs*, Fall 2013.

America blame faceless agencies for the inefficiencies that plague commercial and social life. But in fact it is special-interest manipulation of Congress that has deliberately weakened sound technocratic regulation and made day-to-day affairs less orderly and predictable. The return of professional bureaucracies and their independent leadership is a plea to rescue governance from politics. Restoring the divide between politics and administration, between democratic practice and governance execution, is essential to resurrect Washington's credibility. If government service can be restored to a vocation rather than a lucrative hobby, elected leaders can work with functional agencies to ensure that policies and` institutions are designed to maximize welfare and anticipate demands.

Congress does not have to be a body shaped solely by the whims of populism or special interests. The Congressional Research Service (CRS), which responds to queries from specific committees or members, could be empowered as a preparatory body to shape legislation and keep it within the realm of the rational. Congress's options would be narrowed to those which benefit the maximum number of citizens rather than those most favored by industry lobbies. The Government Accountability Office (GAO) and Congressional Budget Office (CBO) are other examples of legislative branch bodies that provide quality assessments that should more regularly inform important decisions such as scenarios for the spending of additional oil and gas export revenues. Unfortunately, former House speaker Newt Gingrich's anti-government bias led to Congressional staff being massively slashed. Meanwhile, professionals have been replaced by outside contractors who have less experience but actually cost more. Today, even as the world gets more complex, Congress is just winging it.

Another way to keep politicians in touch with the people is to have only a part-time legislature. In the late 18th and early 19th century, America had part-time Congressmen who made irregular visits to Washington. That is a tradition that continues today in Switzerland and Singapore, both of whose parliamentarians maintain professional careers that keep them grounded in the real world. They can neither leverage their offices to hoard money with impunity nor can they afford poor performance that impacts their reputations in society. They have to look their constituents directly in the eyes on a daily basis—and explain to them why a policy does or doesn't conform to their wishes.

Deliberative efforts now abound in America, but they are parallel civic programs, not directly linked to real legislative processes. The Aspen Institute's Pluribus project, for example, aspires to articulate the views of apathetic non-voters, while James Fishkin of Stanford has led productive deliberative polling experiments to bring voters towards more convergent positions on hot-button issues like gun control. But absent direct input into law-making, this is mere social tinkering, powerless in the face of special interests. Can we imagine an era where democracy can be conducted through real-time deliberation and direct citizen input in policy-making, in which indirect Congressional representation is unnecessary?

Constant Contact: Democracy as Data

There could hardly be a more pro-democratic technocratic measure than mandatory voting. Rather than politicians getting elected with 30 percent of the total voting-age population's approval, mandatory voting guarantees a demographically inclusive process, and eventually a more informed populace as well.[18] The US could save itself billions of dollars in voter registration drives, mechanical polling booths and other Election Day drama if American citizens at home and abroad had a one-week window to cast their votes electronically through a secure online portal. Estonia has had national Internet voting since 2005, while e-voting is currently being rolled out across Switzerland. Leapfrogging to direct digital democracy is a simple matter of passing a mandatory voting law plus building an app.

But elections are retroactive, they often punish rather than prescribe. Because they are a referendum on individuals as much as issues, they don't provide citizen guidance on specific policies. Voting alone is therefore far from the best means of capturing popular sentiment on an ongoing basis about the vast range of issues that concern citizens.

For that we need data: Qualitative data such as surveys, polls and social media, and quantitative data such as demographic and economic trends. Data can be more comprehensive than election results for it is broader in scope (covering the full spectrum of issues rather than being hijacked by hot-button topics) and fresher (collected more regularly than infrequent elections). Scaling technology is easier than scaling trust, but the former can be a path to the latter. More substantive interactions—even virtual ones—between citizens and politicians could make a massive contribution toward reducing the trust gap in American politics.

Data-driven direct technocracy is superior to representative

---

18 Voter turnout in both presidential and parliamentary elections has declined worldwide from an average of 85 percent to about 60 percent between 1970 and 2014.

democracy because it dynamically captures the specific desires of the people while short-circuiting the distortions of elected representatives, special interests and corrupt middlemen. This is not the antithesis of bucolic notions of free-spirited yet considered public deliberation (which, in any case, is far more a Swiss reality than an American idea). To the contrary, data tools give citizens the full range of information they need to make decisions on issues on an ongoing basis. In Switzerland, democracy is not something that is done for the people by representatives; they co-create and co-design policies. This means that the frequent Swiss initiatives and referenda are not lesser events in between more important elections; they are a form of habitual voting on all issues of importance. In fact, the Swiss are so confident in their direct democracy that citizens have come to consider parliament itself an irritating intermediary—and recently floated an initiative to abolish it entirely.

Constant adaptation to new technologies is a hallmark of the info-state. Today we think of data tools as aiding democracy, but eventually, democratic deliberation (whether elections, initiatives, surveys, or social media) become contributing data-sets among many that together help technocrats steer policy. For example, data that represents the unrepresented (those who don't actively vote or participate in surveys)—such as their financial behavior and education status—are essential inputs for leaders to ensure they are taking everyone's needs into account. Data also helps to balance what people want with what is good for them. Everyone may want free sugary drinks, but nobody wants to pay for the bloated (pardon the pun) healthcare system that will result.

The info-state shouldn't be ruled by data, but balance data and democracy so they complement each other: Data can determine which policies are necessary, while democracy can modify and ratify them. A new generation of data tools can encourage more reasoned discourse through presenting accurate information and realistic scenarios. Building on its now infamous Watson platform, IBM's new Debating Technologies search massive troves of research to generate and concisely summarize the pro and con positions on thorny issues such as pipeline projects, tax policy, and the regulation of violent video games. When data becomes part of the language of deliberation, democracy becomes more more rational rather than overly emotive.

Singapore is pioneering a new model of constant consultation based equally on democracy and data. Parliamentarians hold weekly "meet the people" sessions in community centers to collect views and feedback on the budget, housing policy, healthcare and other issues. Detailed questionnaires are circulated to the public to produce what is now called "Census Plus," giving the government better data with which to plan future mixed-use housing and commercial developments as well as public subways and bus routes, ultimately reducing vehicle demand. Consultation with citizens, experts, businesses, NGOs and social groups is essential for the legitimacy and success of all regimes, democratic or authoritarian. It is how knowledge is crowdsourced and how local nuance can prevail over blanket doctrines.

At the same time, the Big Data of complex and often unstructured information can generate correlations and projections from which policymakers can derive scenarios. With the completion of a nation-wide fiber optic Internet roll-out, Singapore's physical sensor network ("Internet of Things") provides enormous volumes of data on, for example, vehicular and traffic flows or electricity consumption, so that relevant agencies can adjust streetlights and boost power capacity during peak demand periods to avoid outages. As civil service head Peter Ong reminds, "The goal is not just better predictions, but better decisions."

The US has not yet evolved this far. Democrats and Republicans view data as little more than a political weapon. Census data, for example, has enabled political parties to pinpoint messages for constituents right down to the street and block level. Newt Gingrich famously claimed that the Democrats won the 2008 election because they "had better data." By 2012, Obama's campaign CTO Harper Reed and his team had a geo-located electoral database enabling them to conduct predictive polling and messaging targeting women, white males, Latinos, the elderly, or other key voter groups. Republicans learned their lesson. Armed with more precise maps of electoral geography, they have used their House majority to aggressively gerrymander districts in Democratic states such as Wisconsin, Pennsylvania, Michigan, and Florida. As the Democrats' voter base grew, its number of seats shrank.

Census data combined with a gerrymandered map points America's political parties to the half-dozen swing states and districts within them that decide entire national elections. Judging from the campaigns, one would think that all of America looks like the Rust Belt districts of Michigan, Ohio and Pennsylvania. But America is not Detroit. Twice as many Americans wake up each morning in the "gigonomy" of digital freelancers than work in factories. Surely the professional needs and aspirations of 80 million millennials should register as an election issue?

Data should be a pathway to better policy, not just the next arms race between political parties. One way to accomplish this is through more data on government itself. Civic initiatives such as GovTrack and Project Vote Smart allow anyone to go online and view in real-time all legislative sessions, bills up for authorization, statements made in hearings, voting records of Congressmen and, crucially, all available financial records of their campaign contributions. Such public-disclosure campaigns strengthen the hands of citizens to ensure their priorities are addressed. When survey data reveals that the elderly require greater diversity in medical programs, and youth more educational options, the result must be more than talking points for election campaign speeches but the implementation of policies to address needs. A more digital society advances transparency in the service of accountability, without which democracy is just chatter.

America's former CTO Todd Park and his successor Megan Smith have been strong advocates of integrating data tools into government agencies both to streamline them and encourage data-sharing across them. They also oversee a new Digital Service Corps of young tech talent on sabbatical from the IT industry who are the boots on the ground of integrating new technologies into old bureaucracies. (From Harvard's Kennedy School to Oxford's Blavatnik School, new curricula are being developed around digital governance to train the next generation of "datacrats.") But even as they have tried to make federal services such as Obamacare and veterans affairs more efficient, they have faced enormous bureaucratic barriers, multiple data systems across agencies and conflicts across federal and state lines that have together ensured that national e-government remains a distant dream.

Given the widely cited decline in civic associations in America today—gatherings where, as Tocqueville put it, "people look at something other than themselves"—social media should become ever more a strategic tool for gathering knowledge about citizens' priorities. After all, Tocqueville didn't see democracy as a tool to enhance belonging to a particular community but rather as an ethos of individual freedom, the right to choose and participate in all manner of associations. Should popular sentiments always be filtered through the geographic lens of political constitutencies when society has become so physically and digitally mobile? Americans are social creatures—Washington should pay attention to what they say in their new digital communities.

At present, however, it is technocracies like Singapore are adapting faster to the need for digital democracy than traditional democracies are. Western polemicists used to argue that communications and social media technologies would make Chinese authoritarianism obsolete once everyone had access to mobile phones, satellite TV, and other information channels. But in fact it is challenging the mandates of unresponsive democratic leaders while *reinforcing* the legitimacy of technocratic regimes that are responsive to public needs and demands.

No doubt governments can gain intrusive powers by manipulating, tracking and censoring Internet access—but the Internet does not bolster their legitimacy unless it is used to acknowledge and respond to public concerns. China's Internet policy is a mix of restraint and embrace. Chinese censors block undesired Internet content from within and outside (the so-called "Great Firewall"). At the same time, Chinese authorities monitor Weibo and WeChat's 700 million plus users' microblogs and messages in real-time to pinpoint and prosecute corruption. (They also punish websites that spread false rumors.) Party officials even host discussion forums on Weibo, and have invited online petitioning.

Beijing listens closely to criticism and even dissent, even as it restricts collective demonstrations of resistance. This is not democracy, but it represents a gradual expansion of the scope of accountability in places where rule has otherwise been far more arbitrary.

In China, the ruling Party already has an internal social media platform for gathering ideas and building policy coalitions. It also gets consistent advice from the diverse committees of the People's Political Consultative Conference, whose members include hundreds of notable figures from business and society. In 2013 alone, new inductees included Baidu chairman Robin Li, actor Jackie Chan, basketball great Yao Ming, and Nobel laureate in literature Mo Yan. Scholar Zhang Weiwei describes the role of the Consultative Conference as helping the Party assess the *minxin* (hearts and minds of the people) versus the fleeting and contradictory *minyi* (public opinion).

In *Why Nations Fail*, scholars Daron Acemoglu and James Robinson argue that in the long run, inclusive political systems deliver stability and growth better than non-inclusive ones. While their statements indicate a preference for Western democracy, their own evidence points to China as an exception to their rule. Rather than bending—or ignoring—practice to suit theory, academics should take note of the ways in which countries such as China practice various forms of consultation and representation to gauge and respond to citizen preferences. China's system is not democratic, but its resilience is a testament to its inclusiveness.

From Parties to Coalitions

Even with a greater role for civic consultation and data in political deliberation, America still needs to majorly reform its political party structures to channel those insights into law-making that reflects public sentiment. The particular form of legislature best suited to the info-state is a multi-party parliament. Almost all of the almost two dozen countries that rank ahead of the US in indicators ranging from civil rights to government functionality are parliamentary systems where the executive emerges from the parliament. The prime minister comes from its ranks, but he also must confront his peers. He cannot hide behind the white walls of executive privilege. In a parliamentary system, the government's feet are always held to the fire. Failure to meet key benchmarks in reasonable timeframes can lead to no-confidence votes and trigger elections faster than in America's rigidly staggered election cycles. These can either be general elections or just leadership changes within the governing party. Australia has certainly had an alarming number of elections in recent years, but at least they are not stuck with unpopular leaders for a day longer than necessary.

Multi-party parliamentary systems either have a single-party majority or a coalition of two or more parties that agree on their platform and can get things done. Because parliamentary systems are not American-style winner-take-all, the leading party—and prime minister—still has to create a cabinet that fairly reflects the balance of parties and build consensus across a parliamentary coaltion. In Britain, David Cameron required a coalition with the smaller Liberal Democratic Party to oust Labour leader Tony Blair in 2010. But by the 2015 general election, the government had delivered on reducing the deficit and Cameron's conservatives won an outright majority. After the UK's June 2016 "Brexit" vote, Theresa May became Britain's prime minister after David Cameron resigned and other contenders dropped out. Clearly she was not directly elected by the people, but both her own majority Tory party and the Labour opposition can challenge her mandate and call for elections. This is a reminder that parliamentary systems better balance of positions and personalities than the American government. Technically, voters don't know who the prime minister will be until after an election when coalitions are formed and the party has selected its leader.

With a science PhD and no-nonsense attitude, Germany's Angela Merkel is Europe's parliamentary technocrat par excellence. As chancellor since 2005, Merkel began with the slimmest of electoral margins and had to forge a "Grand Coalition" with her CDU party's great rival, the social-democratic SPD. In 2013 Merkel's CDU won again, but its traditional preferred partner the FDP—with which it had governed since 2009—failed to win enough seats to enter parliament at all, so the *Grosse Koalition* returned and continues into the present. (The abbreviation "GroKo" even became the country's word of the year in 2013.) Germany shoulders a greater burden than any other European nation, and yet its coalitions have been able to manage the hot-button domestic issues of unemployment, immigration and taxation while also holding the Eurozone together.

In parliamentary systems, the government cannot be at permanent loggerheads because the failure to pass legislation results in dismissal of parliament and the calling of fresh elections. Either legislators get things done or the people actually throw them out quickly. Indeed, parliamentary systems also have very short election cycles of 2 to 3 months in which candidates mobilize and have fixed public budgets for campaigning. Comparing this to America's nearly two years and $1-billion-plus electoral circus is reason enough to consider an overhaul of the American political system. Related to this, without America's long lame-duck election periods, coalitions offer forward momentum rather than stasis; they shake themselves up regularly rather than playing chicken and shutting down the government. A comparison of European and American road intersections illustrates the point by analogy. European countries have more roundabouts than traffic signals; cars are always moving, and only slow down to change direction or streets. They consume less fuel and have fewer traffic jams. America uses more stoplights, which result in long lines or force cars to wait on red even when there are no other vehicles in the vicinity.

Parliamentary systems without a strong civil service are still more representative of the populace, but are not necessarily more effective. For example, Canada ranks higher than the US on the EIU's Quality of Democracy Index, but as Alison Loat and Michael Macmillan document in their insightful recollection *Tragedy of the Commons*, Canada's parliamentarians come into office knowing almost nothing about federal politics. What they do learn, however—as in the English parliamentary system they have inherited—is pointless shenanigans like minority backbenchers blocking colleagues from voting while the session's clock ticks down. Meanwhile, Canada's upper house, the Senate, is much like Britain's House of Lords, a useless bastion of unelected privilege. To the extent that anything gets done, it in closed door, multi-party committees where effectiveness rather than partisanship is rewarded. (This is how prime minister Paul Martin managed to slash the country's ballooning deficit in the 1990s.) Still, given the recent years of electoral sideswipes, Canada's new prime minister Justin Trudeau isn't taking any chances. Despite his political inexperience—or perhaps because of it—he has chosen the technocratic path by setting up parallel advisory committees of experts to focus on complex issues such as climate change and infrastructure.

America needs to evolve towards a multi-party system as a first step towards a more genuinely representative legislature. There are two kinds of populism in America: Anti-government and anti-rich. The anti-government is represented by Donald Trump and the anti-rich by Bernie Sanders. Both movements effectively usurped the complacent party base, a stark reminder that neither party represents the large segment of Americans who are socially liberal and fiscally conservative. Indeed, 42 percent of voters now identify as independent, party-agnostic, or even anti-party. A 2013 poll of Tea Party members found that two-thirds of them disapproved of Republicans—so why are they part of the Republican party?

Given this gap between existing structures and public preferences, it seems logical that the Tea Party, Libertarian Party, Green Party and potentially others should emerge as formal national players if they are able to attain a threshold number of seats (say, five). This would give them a real role in policy discourse rather than merely staging rallies every four years. Adding a third (and fourth) party to America's legislature would be a major bulwark against Congress's complacent stagnation. These parties would not only contest district elections and thus force Democrats and Republicans to earn their "safe seats." They would also push citizens' agendas in Congress in ways established parties ignore. Of course, this is precisely what a money-driven two-party system will stop at nothing to prevent.

But America's 80 million millennials aren't accustomed to binary choices. Congress should evolve with the times.

Governors over Senators

The US Senate too is powered by inertia—it is the way it is because that is how it has been. It's broke but let's not bother to fix it. The Senate was designed as an aristocratic check on popular will as embodied in the House, which Tocqueville observed was a bastion of "petty passions." Indeed, for over a century, only the House of Representatives was directly elected while the Senate served as a safe space from populism. But the 17th amendment (ratified in 1913) subjected senators to direct elections, reducing their autonomy. Gradually, they have become as much the self-serving operators as Representatives are. The fact that some Senators have been legendary brokers of compromise masks the reality that the upper house too has become just another partisan redoubt, an arcane body focused mostly on managing its own antiquated procedures—such as filibusters to block votes and secret holds to block nominations—with equal or greater effort given to fundraising for reelection.

Since more than half the Senate is now comprised of former congressmen rather than experienced governors (as was the case in the past), it the gravitas it was created to provide in addressing big national priorities like healthcare and financial reform, foreign affairs and trade. A proper overhaul of the legislative branch would therefore do nothing less than replace the Senate entirely with the members of the National Governors Association, creating a Governors Assembly. America's governors actually run their states, oversee large bureaucracies, manage complex budgets, and understand local realities. Senators *talk and debate* about the novel experiments in healthcare and worker training going on in their states; governors actually *create and run* them. Unlike squabbling senators, governors get along extremely well with each other and overwhelmingly favor cross-border projects that enhance their connectivity to each other. Rather than each state having two senators, it should have two governors—either running on a joint ticket, or with the two most popular candidates being chosen. After the election, one will work in the state capital and the other in Washington coordinating priorities and agendas and sharing successful policies with their peers from other states. Especially since Senate rules have barely evolved in 200 years, this would at least ensure fewer filibusters and more actual policy.

Let's not get held up on the notion that the Senate has a constitutional duty to vote on matters such as Supreme Court justices. The Senate's role is "advice and consent," which in present times has translated into holding hostage nominations for everyone from ambassadors to justices until the president bends on an unrelated matter. All branches of government would be better off without extortion being passed off as checks and balances—not least the judicial branch itself.

The Rules of Law

The framers and architects of America's Constitution were an assemblage of legislators, scholars and citizens who drafted, redrafted and re-re-drafted the legal foundations of the confederation. Why has the drafting stopped? For one thing, amending the constitution requires the kind of super-majority at the Congressional and state level that is nearly impossible to imagine in today's divisive climate. There hasn't been a meaningful amendment to the Constitution since the 26th amendment lowered the voting age to 18 in 1971. At the same time, America still clings to the 2nd amendment two centuries after its intent was fulfilled: To protect state militias, not to enshrine individual rights to semi-automatic weapons. By contrast, Germany's constitution is not treated as a sacred Bible to be dogmatically obeyed but a living document able to adapt to the times. Germany regularly amends its constitution (the "Basic Law" known as the *Grundgesetz*) to recognize more national languages, increase the mandate for social services provision, re-regulate the role of police or strengthen protection of privacy.

For a constitution to not become a relic, it has to enter the Wikipedia age. The correct way to approach delicate subjects of long-term significance such as constitutional amendments is through the formation of impartial parliamentary committees devoted to consulting experts, reviewing international case studies and benchmarks, and modeling consequences. Iceland's most recent constitution was widely described as a crowd-sourced "Wiki" constitution developed over a four month period with widespread public participation via social media, but in fact it was continuously being drafted and revised by a special parliamentary committee that included elements derived from this substantial citizen consultation. Again, democracy and technocracy hand-in-hand.

Unfortunately, even America's most nominally independent bodies are heading in the opposite direction. The appointment of justices itself has become a morbidly partisan exercise: Hope a justice of the opposite political leaning dies on your watch so you can appoint a successor with your ideological leaning.

Republican grandstanding after the sudden death of justice Antonin Scalia challenged even this convention, claiming that any Obama-appointed successor would be illegitimate. They got their way: President Trump will likely preside over at least three Supreme Court appointments.

There are numerous ways to reverse the utterly contingent nature of the Supreme Court appointment process, and indeed that for all federal judges. The president could appoint a diverse panel of lawmakers, lawyers and experts to make merit-based recommendations from which the president would choose as vacancies arise (as Jimmy Carter did). Justices could serve for a single term of ten years, ensuring a steady rotation of energy and ideas. When it comes to confirmations, it's odd that a successful Supreme Court nominee is s/he who says as little as possible about his or her actual views—"taking the Fifth," as it were. Why not have candidates clearly articulate their positions on Constitutional issues, and even what amendments they feel are necessary to improve the functioning of the court and the Constitution's relevance to society?

There is little debate that the purpose of the Supreme Court is to uphold the Constitution and protect the rights of all citizens, but why wait for the happenstance of case selection to determine what America's view is on the right to privacy, or to decide on the role of technology in evidence collection? There are several ways high courts can contribute to the evolution of governance beyond the interpretations embedded in specific case rulings. As Anne-Marie Slaughter argued over a decade ago in *A New World Order*, courts have become part of the inter-governmental network of agencies that actively harmonize laws to smooth the flows of people and commerce. As the US and EU (and their companies) continuously find themselves at odds over IP protection and individual data privacy (such as with the Safe Harbour and Privacy Shield disputes), their courts should be speaking to each other to anticipate the implications of new technologies and plan for the regulatory consequences rather than waiting for corporate lawsuits. The world's services economy is growing much faster than the goods economy, and courts can make sure the pie continues to grow rather than let the Internet get Balkanized.

Smart courts—along with smart legislatures—also actively benchmark their policies against those of others and compare the outcomes. The wealth of international experience in legal and policy matters can be coded into databases for all nations to access, allowing them to consider all options and consequences. It should be seen as a sign of our political evolution that we choose not to willfully repeat mistakes that have been made by others.

What America has done, however, is to over-legislate such that an endless layering of statutory laws now overwhelms both common law and the autonomous ability of courts to govern by following pragmatic reason. This is the new legal red tape. Noted legal scholar Philip Howard, author of *The Death of Common Sense* and *Rule of Nobody*, argues that the millions of pages of federal laws smack of Soviet-era central planning. The simplest matters such as permits for construction projects require legal procedures that can ultimately double project costs. His advocacy movement Common Good champions technocratic fixes such as a one-stop shop for business permits as well as civic solutions such as appointing an independent council of citizens that recommend commissions for simplifying laws.[19]

This is a better use of citizens' time than serving on juries. Unless you are regularly hauled into court for burglary, drunk driving or other criminal offenses, your interaction with the legal system comes in the form of the dreaded jury summons. In America it's frequently heard that jury duty is an essential ingredient of democracy, promoting civic virtue and a sense of fairness. This is yet another notion that makes for sonorous theory but in practice is a giant waste of time compared to far more efficient modes of dispensing justice. Criminal courts are not the Model United Nations; watching "Judge Judy" does not make one qualified to navigate courtroom complexity and weigh evidence. European countries such as Germany and France have so-called "mixed tribunals" in which a small handful of citizens (often just two or three), either laypersons or experts, are appointed or selected to assess cases alongside a panel of expert judges. Taxpayers are spared the ludicrous cost of the banalities of jury selection (such as lottery wheels to select jurors) which turn American justice into a mix of reality show and kangaroo court.

---

19 Howard also suggests a number of constitutional amendments such as forced sunset within 15 years for all laws that have budgetary impact, line-item veto authority for the president over Congressional budgets, and full presidential authority over executive branch personnel.

For a high-res version of this infographic, please visit:
http://www.paragkhanna.com/home/2016/10/18/technocracy-in-america

5.
CALL IN THE TECHNOCRATS

Getting Our House in Order

Foreign observers of the US are perpetually amazed by America's dynamism and resilience—traits unlike those of any other large society. And yet they also comment with equal certainty that American politics guarantees it will squander some of its best opportunities. Unless we are to celebrate policy failure for its own sake, we need more technocracy to balance our democracy. As the brilliant political theorist Rahul Sagar writes in his forthcoming book *Decent Regimes*, "brute facts" such as losing a major war compel the sober shift to technocracy. Indeed, after Napoleon III's humiliating defeat by Bismarck's Prussia in 1870, France established the elite Sciences Po to train future political and diplomatic elites. To lift America out of the crushing circumstances of the Depression, Roosevelt's New Deal created large professional bureaucracies such as the Social Security Administration and Fannie Mae to cope with the scale of functions necessary to govern a growing industrial population across a large country. Truman's Federal Highway Administration was a post–World War II example of policy transcending politics as well—you shouldn't half-build a road.

Many of the functions that are necessary for a free, orderly and secure society require the kind of policy continuity that should put them beyond the scope of political manipulation. In the many areas where it is clear what is in the national interest, technocracy helps to drive a wedge between democracy and corrosive politics. The most strategic issues affecting America's future—immigration and education, defense spending and trade policy, healthcare and infrastructure—all require technocratic approaches rather than fact-free populism. When the margin for error shrinks to zero, it always becomes time to call in the technocrats.

In recent years, technocrats have been elevated to resolve serious political dilemmas, only to see their work over-powered by parochial politics. In 2012, the Simpson-Bowles committee was convened to resolve the Congressional budget impasse. Its recommendations, not surprisingly, were ignored. Thus despite a plummeting deficit, we still perennially risk government shutdowns. In a technocracy, the Simpson-Bowles recommendations would not be re-circulated back for approval to the same deadlocked body that brought about the budget crisis in the first place.

Detroit's bankruptcy is another example of technocracy to the rescue—almost. In 2013, Kevyn Orr was appointed by Michigan governor Rick Snyder as an emergency manager to get the city out of receivership, with the authority to change budgets, renegotiate labor contracts, privatize services and cut long-term deals with investors. His powers amounted to the suspension of democracy, but eventually day-to-day operations of the city were handed back to mayor Mike Duggan. Given the state of Detroit and other failing Michigan towns, however, one cannot expect technocrats to be miracle workers.

Detroit's salvation lies in a broader national infrastructural rehabilitation—the equivalent of Truman's Federal Highway Administration—a $3.6 trillion program put forth by the American Society of Civil Engineers. In addition to the millions of "shovel ready" jobs such an undertaking would create, it would also prepare America to become the country of 400 million residents it is on course to be by 2050. With interest rates near zero, trillions of dollars in corporate assets sitting on the sidelines, and hundreds of billions in foreign investment coming in annually, there has never been a better time to launch a National Infrastructure Bank (NIB), something Congress has talked about but dithered on for a decade. There must be something fundamental about infrastructure if it is the only thing Hillary Clinton and Donald Trump agreed on.

Yet because Congress thinks in terms of districts and states rather than industries and supply chains, it shortchanges any long-term infrastructure program. Even the Department of Transportation still requires separate spending proposals from all 50 states rather than encouraging regional plans across state boundaries that would stimulate more efficient commerce. It is as if Thomas Jefferson's 200-year-old map of America—in which states were designed to have relatively equal size to maintain a balance of power—matters more than the reality of 350 metro-regions in desperate need of greater connectivity to each other.

What is more, America's political divides result from these connectivity divides: Political leanings are no longer between "red state" and "blue state" but between high-density and low-density geographies, the former overwhelmingly Democrat and liberal and the latter Republican and conservative. The fact that America is the least urbanized of Western societies, combined with the anachronistic electoral college system, together account for America's deep socio-political division and Trump's victory. Here is what to do if you want to "make America great again" while healing the massive divides running across its map: Build a road.

A technocratic economic system would also spot the glaring inequities in the distribution of post-financial-crisis bail-out funds and adjust the contradictory regulations that incentivized banks to hoard capital rather than lend it to small businesses. It would mandate affordable low-interest-rate home mortgage financing and offer tax breaks to companies for large-scale job-creating or skill-building investments. Smart governments also focus less on raising taxes on companies than on attracting investment from them. Yet a decade after the financial crisis, success in these areas remains anecdotal rather than systematic, the kind of results that a utilitarian technocracy would not tolerate. Especially now that American corporates hold an estimated $5 trillion of cash offshore, missing the chance to lay out clear incentives for repatriation of capital and attracting fresh investment should be considered corrupt negligence.

Beyond the irony that financial institutions remain "too big to fail" and that predatory mortgage practices remain widespread is the fact that these newer kinds of macro-prudential regulations actually represent a better monitoring framework for commercial conduct that provides simple rules that can be interpreted by officials. The growing role of FINRA as an efficient arbitrator of disputes between registered financial brokers and clients, with three-person expert panels making binding decisions without the need for costly public court proceedings, represents another smart technocratic solution to the otherwise overly litigious American norm.

America faces significant structural challenges during the coming demographic transition, with 40 million baby-boomers entering retirement. Most of them have grossly insufficient savings, while pensions are under-funded and returns on savings effectively zero (and this after retirement savings were slashed by the financial crisis). If left to today's democratic lawmakers, the solution might be found once most of them are dead. America's most progressive conversations—and that is all they are at the moment, conversations—around wage insurance are already policy in countries like Denmark, where workers are protected and "rehabilitation teams" are deployed to counsel aging workers on what skills they can continue to use during deferred retirement years.

Similarly, it is all the rage to talk about universal basic income (UBI), as if the funding for such a European style scheme will materialize overnight. A more technocratic US government would establish a combination of a minimum wage and wage supports so that a greater proportion of the citizenry can stay off welfare, pay down their enormous credit card debt, and contribute to more balanced consumption in the economy. Technocracies know that such investments effectively pay for themselves in commerce, tax revenue, and a healthier and less violent society.

Healthcare is another obvious candidate for more technocratic approaches. Sweden convened an independent committee of experts to reform its healthcare system, mandating lower costs for services, performance based pay for doctors, and other measures that immediately slashed 35 percent off its healthcare budget while improving care for the population. Sweden lets markets deliver, but prescribes standards and costs to ensure access and opportunity for its people. Obamacare has been an effort at the latter but without adequate regulation of the former.

Health science stands out as an another obvious case study in policy that should be kept out of ignorant politicians' reach. In an aging society, greater research into disease prevention and affordable pharmaceuticals is more essential than ever. Yet Congress has been cutting National Institutes of Health (NIH) funding which underwrites large capital expenditures in laboratories that do such cutting-edge medical research.

Immigration and education are other national concern ripe for technocratic intervention. America is a land of immigrants that has welcomed millions of foreigners, rich and poor, talented and unskilled. It has lured the best and brightest to places like Silicon Valley, and even re-exported them to launch places like Bangalore. About half of America's tech companies are founded or run by immigrants, especially from India and China. And yet America's restrictive immigration policy even towards highly skilled engineers has frustrated the tech sector's efforts to recruit more talented programmers from abroad, leading many of them to migrate elsewhere and work for rival firms. Tech companies such as Facebook, Google and LinkedIn have thus formed their own PAC called *FWD.us* to lobby for raising the H1B visa quota. The technocratic solution to immigration, of course, would look much different. Work visas would be issued much more readily based on employer demand from critical industries, with fast-track citizenship for those who maintain solid performance. That is the difference between immigration gridlock and immigration *planning*.

Education policy faces a similar mix of chaos and malaise. Many think the country is in the midst of a dynamic rebalancing between an ossified public school system and progressive, results-oriented charter schools. But in fact the system is just splintering America further while overall results lag behind other advanced countries. Building an educated middle class is a national responsibility—an an essential ingredient of successful democracy. Experimentation is important, but it cannot alone lift the floor. Similarly, a technocracy would not need two decades to debate whether or not to have some kind of national service program for high school graduates that helps them find their way while building civic solidarity—only to not create one.

America's high school graduates lack the technical competence for the future skills economy. A century ago, America's most common job was farmer. Today it is retail salesperson or truck driver. With both of these likely to be automated away to robots and autonomous vehicles, now would be a good time for the departments of Labor and Commerce to develop a job-creation strategy for the redundant and under-skilled (especially since many states with growing tech sectors such as North Carolina don't have enough workers to replace the current wave of retirees).

Of course, American workers have been promised retraining programs at least since when John Edwards—remember him?—was running for president. But while Congress has been busy renaming public squares after Chinese dissidents, companies such as IBM and Starbucks have stepped in to set up their own institutes and partner with community colleges to shape associate-degree programs to up-skill graduates for the jobs they need, immediately hiring thousands of such trainees. Do such stopgap measures really enable the US to compete with a country like Germany, where industry associations, universities and the government collaborate on an ongoing basis to introduce the most relevant technical curricula to keep their students' skills at the cutting edge? Americans have invented many of the disruptions that are threatening their own employment base. It would be a pity for Americans to be among the last to take advantage of them. Yet today it is extremely difficult to imagine America's democratic process generating a strategy to harness the disruptions of techno-capitalism for broad social benefit.

Technocrats can make big, unpopular and painful decisions that are also urgent, necessary and even essential for national wellbeing. That does not necessarily mean top-down decision-making but rather encouraging local experimentation and searching for successful models to scale. For decades experts have recommended amnesty for illegal aliens and legalization of marijuana, ideas taboo at the national level but gaining ground in progressive states that now serve as national role models. An info-state would gather evidence from local experiments, modify policies to improve them and spread best practices. While many states may wish to maintain regressive policies, the task of a utilitarian government is to protect all citizens from prejudice. This means revisiting the 10th amendment rather than waiting for cases to land before the Supreme Court, which often cites that amendment when it passes decisions back down to the states. Either America's states learn from each other—and the government encourages that evolution—or it isn't really a United States.

The United Info-States of America

At no point in the past decade has any official or academic in a foreign country told me they want their country to look like "America." They want to have a Silicon Valley, a New York City and a Boston—hubs of innovation, finance, and knowledge. (California hosts almost one thousand foreign dignitaries per year.) If they can, they limit their Washington visits to a day or two before dashing off to see what they can learn from America's leading nodes.

America's historical resilience is owed to its geopolitical security, distributed geography, stable currency, entrepreneurial culture and many other virtues that fortunately survive despite its dysfunctional political system. But it shouldn't push its luck. While America is far larger either in population or per capita wealth (or both) than any other country of comparable geographic size—Russia, Canada, China, Brazil, India, Australia—the New Deal spirit of national unity has given way to a return to de facto federalism in which many states and cities are on their own. While America has more large, wealthy, diverse and connected cities than any other country, a great deal more needs to be done to future-proof 350 million people spread across 350 major metro areas.

A number of American states have natural or historical advantages playing out in their favor. Texas and Nevada, for example, have energy or gambling revenues that allow them to eliminate income taxes and attract millions of new residents to their cheap land and homes and sunny weather. Washington State also has no income tax but levies higher housing and other taxes to pay for new infrastructure projects and key social services.

Seattle leads the way in shifting its building regulations towards smaller micro-apartments for the single-person households that represent more than half the national population. Staying indoors becomes cramped; people have to go out to socialize and find jobs, creating a more dynamic city environment.

California has no doubt had its up and downs: Initially a standard-setter in statewide infrastructure, universities and emissions regulation, massive budgetary imbalances ensued as citizens refused to raise property taxes while relentlessly voting for more spending. By 2011, Standard & Poor's rated California the worst run state in America. Jerry Brown's return as governor restored fiscal sanity with higher taxes on the rich and debt-conscious zero-based budgeting. Brown's top-down mandates co-exist with innovations in California's balloting and referenda system. As in Switzerland, California citizens have a direct voice in everything from sales tax to driverless cars to cell phone kill switches. While ballot initiatives have sometimes been narrow and confusing (and the requisite number of signatures collected through bribes), they are now being structured to work with the state legislature rather than around it. As of 2014, state lawmakers gather one month before an initiative ballot is launched to make clarifications and compromises, and ballots will clearly indicate the financial sponsors of each measure. Furthermore, voter initiatives will soon be migrated entirely online. If California can manage immigration, education, irrigation and transportation, it could become America's largest info-state.

The American political system is ill-designed to collectively navigate a hyper-competitive global landscape in which each American state competes as much with its neighbors as with foreign countries. But it has long been the case that innovation comes from sub-state provinces and cities such as Silicon Valley. Indeed, when Michael Porter wrote *The Competitive Advantage of Nations*, he focused not just on small states such as New Zealand, the Netherlands and Taiwan, but also on sub-state provinces like the Basque region of Spain and Massachusetts. Competition breeds innovation: America should become a union of info-states.

The US now has multiple high-tech hubs including Silicon Valley, Boston, New York and Washington, DC—each of which has competitive advantages in areas such as computing, defense, data analytics, and biotech. At well over $10 billion per year, America's venture capital pool is by far the world's largest—but 75 percent of it is spent in California, New York, and Massachusetts. Far too few states and city-regions have viable economic plans that align government, industry and the education sector to develop specialized industry clusters serving the US and global markets. They need to map out their domestic and international partners and supply chains, and be on a war footing against rivals.

Justice Louis Brandeis famously called states the "laboratories of democracy," but they are also very much the incubators of *technocracy*. Across the country, governors and mayors have realized that the key to their success is devolution: Secure as much independence from Washington as possible and run policies best suited to your state. The virtue of devolution is not only that distributing authority is as powerful a check on tyranny as democracy, but that it allows for local experiments and rapid citizen feedback, resulting in models that the federal government can further study and scale to other states. The paradox of devolution then is that the city can be the ideal site of both democracy *and* technocracy.

Consider that it is much more at the city than national level where third parties can emerge, contest and win elections, as evidenced by America's Green Party, which is far more prominent in local legislatures than at the federal level but fielded medical doctor Jill Stein as a presidential candidate. At the same time, cities are pursuing far more progressive social policies than Congress can wrap its head around. For example, as immigration reform stalls in the Congress, New York City is creating a special Municipal ID as a path towards amnesty for undocumented migrants, bringing this crucial sector of the workforce out of the shadows. It has also begun testing social impact bonds by which companies invest in programs that reduce the likelihood of male prison recidivism by funding training programs that the state later repays while saving massively on the cost of an ever growing incarcerated population. Seattle is now a political innovator as the first city to offer publicly funded vouchers (through a property tax) to political candidates if they agree to limit their spending.

City-level info-states view governance as a hackable organism. Former Mayor Michael Bloomberg set up the New York City Economic Development Corporation (NYCEDC) to lead the charge to make it a "digital city," giving grants to tech incubators and establishing the Center for Urban Science and Progress in Brooklyn, which trains professionals in data analytics. The city's former transportation commissioner Janette Sadik-Khan hired architects from Copenhagen and tracked pedestrian patterns in order to redesign Times Square in a more people-friendly direction. Dan Doctoroff, once Bloomberg's deputy mayor in New York, now spearheads Google Sidewalk, a start-up that began with turning payphones into Wi-Fi hotspots but has grown into a far more extensive suite of apps that use big data from municipal offices, medical records and real-time mobile citizens to better route traffic, plan health clinics and shape land management. Boston, long a hub for everything from fishing to education to finance, has launched an "Urban Mechanics Office" to plan more efficient transport and housing services. While it raises over $2 billion annually just in property taxes, it now co-invests with companies to leverage more capital.

Much more readily than nations, cities have the capacity to reinvent themselves within a single generation. Indeed, some of today's smartest cities are also the oldest cities, especially in Europe. The global community of urban architects and community organizers is largely in agreement that inclusive cities must feature mixed-use, mixed-income neighborhoods that encourage pedestrianism and incorporate multi-use public spaces. If proximity is the hallmark of the sustainable and productive 21st century city, then Europe's medieval and medium-sized cities are well-suited to adapt to the future since most of what people want is within a ten-minute walk of where they live. Indeed, Amsterdam, Barcelona and Berlin are a decade ahead of any American city in sensor-driven traffic management, smart cards, and electric vehicle deployment. European countries are starting to require employers to calculate wages from the start-time of workers' commute, thus altering their policies to be more supportive of both telecommuting and childcare. Such measures are all but impossible in America's sprawling cities with their dilapidated infrastructure. Across Southeast Asia (especially Malaysia and Singapore) one also finds the charmingly convenient shophouse architecture in which the only commute is from upstairs to downstairs. In the coming decade, Singapore will expand this concept to larger-scale mixed-use public housing, with upper levels for housing and lower for retail and social functions. The old can become new faster than the relatively new can.

Despite lacking the density of European and Asian cities, America's urban leaders have tremendous wind in their sails. The country's mayors have a far higher average trust rating than the president, Congress and even the Supreme Court. They set key performance indicators (KPIs) across municipal agencies and leverage social media to communicate in real time with the public. With his raft of KPIs for New York City, Bloomberg lived by the mantra, "If you can't measure it, you can't manage it." No wonder Bloomberg was awarded the Lee Kuan Yew Cities Prize in 2012.

An America with several hundred leaders like Jerry Brown and Michael Bloomberg would need a very different political system than today's district and state-based Congress with its gerrymandering and pork-laden legislation. Democracy in a society of distant citizens and infrequent voting is very different from the emergent democracy for a world that is urban, connected, and vocal. American technocracy therefore isn't about centralization but rather supporting devolved democracy.

The great political sociologist Seymour Martin Lipset argued that successful democratic flourishing requires industrialization, urbanization, education and wealth. These conditions are present in today's major cities where citizens have the greatest influence on local policies and decisions. Plato's *polis* was by definition the city-state of ancient Athens, while Rousseau believed that democratic virtue was best advanced in small polities. Tocqueville observed that "municipal independence" was a natural consequence of popular sovereignty. If we want genuine democracy, therefore, we should also want devolution.

Info-states thrive at the intersection of devolution and data.

Devolution changes the *scale* of governance; data changes the *mode* of governance. Devolution leads us to *smaller* units of authority; data gets us more *efficient* authorities. Data-driven political movements that aim to make federal authorities more efficient actually wind up amplifying and accelerating devolutionary pressure. While initiatives such as Data.gov, Code4Gov and Apps4Gov have the noble objective of cleaning-up Washington, no city or state actually *wants* Washington to have more power. They use the same technologies to calculate how much revenue they can keep *from* Washington, and how to substitute for Washington's services. Data thus advances devolution, but devolution makes for more effective democracy. A devolved world of info-states is indeed the surest path to a more genuinely democratic world.

Living Labs Global of Barcelona estimates the world has 557,000 local governments, while the Boston-based NGO Leading Cities' survey of urban executives found that 96 percent of them believe that their problems are very similar to those in other cities. Research by scholar Michele Acuto of University College London demonstrates that there are more than 225 active inter-city learning networks today, greater than the number of inter-governmental organizations. Lessons in governance and sustainability, then, are more transferable across cities than countries, where cultural and historical variables may be more pronounced obstacles to change.

As China becomes ever more a lattice of city-states with a strong central government, it too can leapfrog the Western model of federal democracy by combining more local democratic systems with Beijing's technocratic leadership. The Digital China movement has launched a "Sm@rt City" program to integrate online both citizen services and feedback for a growing roster of cities across the country. Social entrepreneurs have helped Chinese cities set-up online portals for citizens to rate and prioritize projects and liaise directly with mayors' offices. Regulatory experiments have emerged that set competitive standards such as strictly limiting how long cars can stay on the road to curb air pollution. Shanghai is so large that separate policy experiments are run at the district level, such as in the high-rise business hub of Pudong, which alone has about six million residents, and in Puxi, the city's historic center across the Huangpu River.

The notion that western societies rule by reason and eastern societies by despotism is a tired cliché in a world of constant data feedback. The race is not to construct an algorithmic order but a generative algorithm, as in music or architecture, which is interactive and open-ended with infinite possibilities: A structure that does not discriminate against inputs but rather adapts to each change from within the system. Policymaking must therefore become a continuous loop involving stages of assessment, preparation, formulation, implementation, evaluation and modification. It is the society that experiments most without believing in either its own perfection or perfectibility that is most likely to evolve rather than decay.

Maintaining Global Influence

It's fashionable to talk about the impending "collapse of capitalism" in light of rising inequality and environmental degradation. This might make sense were it not for the fact that every single country in the world has become capitalist. The truth is that the main debate is not upstream—whether or not we should have market-based economies—but downstream, *within* capitalism, as to which models are superior between the owners of firms being private actors, government agencies, cooperative enterprises or some hybrid combination. All countries now compete in the same global marketplace in which they seek comparative advantage through industrial policy (subsidies and protection for "national champion" companies), currency manipulation to benefit exports or boosting the role of export credit agencies (ECAs) to gain advantage abroad.

The post-financial crisis rescues and industry bail-outs made clear that America clings to the notion of *laissez faire* capitalism more in theory than practice, but is clearly still struggling to overcome its anti-state reflexes and pursue the strategies that have helped its rivals. Take the Export-Import Bank, whose charter Congress let expire in 2015. GE, one of the bank's perennial beneficiaries, promptly moved 500 power-turbine manufacturing jobs to France, whose export credit agency extended a long-term line of credit to the company to woo it over. The move also helped GE gain approval from French regulators to take over French conglomerate Alstom's power business. America's companies clearly know better than the government how to operate in the new global capitalist landscape.

The handling of international economic agreements also shows a clear lack of rational cost-benefit calculus in favor of populist posturing. Trade and investment agreements boost American exports and bring trillions of dollars of capital into America that create high-value jobs. Yet to win over rust belt voters, denouncing the proposed Trans-Pacific Partnership (TPP) became a race to the bottom. Congress has also prevented the president from authorizing US participation in major IMF reforms that would enhance America's credibility in international institutions. These are matters of national competitiveness, not political footballs, and while technocratic approaches may be politically controversial, that does not make them any less obvious.

There are also grand strategy questions where technocratic guidance is required. America has just become the world's largest oil and gas producer. Shouldn't it avoid the fate of other large commodity exporters like Australia, Canada and Russia who have failed to create—as smaller and wiser Norway has—a robust sovereign wealth fund to conserve energy revenues for investment in infrastructure or debt reduction?

Diplomacy has historically been the preserve of foreign area experts dedicated to knowledge of specific regional languages and societies. But the intrusion of private campaign financing into presidential politics has turned ambassadorships into prizes handed out to the highest bidder, with dilettantes traipsing into countries they know little about only to resign once their ally in the White House retires or is voted out. Nothing could represent a greater degeneration of the very foundation of modern diplomacy, namely the establishment of a core of professionals whose consistent and routinized interactions maintain stable relations. Diplomacy is a noble profession—the second oldest, as the saying goes—and our most senior diplomats should be selected and promoted based on their expertise and contacts *abroad*, not the amount of money they raise at home.

Managing foreign hotspots would also benefit from less politicization. Both the State Department and a wide spectrum of

American scholars from universities and think-tanks opposed the 2003 Iraq war. Could more technocratic war-gaming, rather than shoot-from-the-hip war mongering, have prevented the last 15 years of foreign policy disasters in the Middle East? The Iran nuclear deal is another example of where foreign policy should not unnecessarily be subject to ideologues or special interest groups masquerading as "democratic accountability." With their records of military service, no doubt senators John McCain and Tom Cotton consider themselves to be credible national security hawks, but they should confine their speeches to the Senate floor and leave issues of the Mideast balance of power to the strategists.

Technocratic decision-making over other key global issues does not mean an end to transparency, but it does mean an increase in expert influence. The Bank of International Settlements (BIS), for example, which provides independent research—and warning—to central banks about the impact of excessive leverage in the financial system, has thought through how to reduce monetary policy volatility better than individual governments have. Listening to such bodies only *after* the next crisis begs the question as to why they were created in the first place.

From immigration to climate change to Internet governance, today's hot-button international issues are actually deep structural challenges in need of long-term strategies. Historical civilizations have collapsed precisely because they fail to develop solutions to complex problems. More sophisticated technocracy is better than praying for global democracy.

CONCLUSION: THE BEND OF HISTORY

In the coming decades, global competition will punish the sentimental. A society that could do something better but doesn't is either stupid or suicidal—or both. For political systems this means less emphasis on democracy and more on good governance. Success is measured by delivering welfare domestically and managing global complexity, not by holding elections. Such pragmatism opens the door to fruitful conversation over improving governance rather than presuming one end-state. Governance is more than a race to efficiency, but no Western government would be worse with a bit more emphasis on technocratic substance over democratic style.

America is still the most powerful nation in the world and home to more than 300 million capable people from all walks of life. For their sake, America needs to learn how to govern itself as a more effective state. We cannot simply assume that because in past generations America has demonstrated a capacity for self-renewal that this will happen again today. Pratap Bhanu Mehta, India's leading political scientist, sees the transitions of the 20th and 21st centuries from pre-modern to modern to postmodern societies playing out in all domains: The economic shift from agricultural to urban services economies, the political shift from citizens as subjects to post-democratic privatization and delivery of public services, and a social shift from local affiliations to nationalism to incentive-based communities. He calls on administrative systems to adapt towards decentralized participation, horizontal or peer accountability, public deliberation, and acceptance of complex identities. This is a tall order—and it's far from clear that America will manage these shifts better than others.

Churchill's dictum that democracy is the worst form of government save for the alternatives must be revised. Direct technocracy is the superior model for 21st century governance. It combines Switzerland's collective presidency executive and multi-party parliament with Singapore's data-driven and utilitarian-minded civil service: A blend of technocracy and democracy, assisted by technology. To keep pace, America doesn't have to reinvent the wheel, but it does have to get on the bandwagon. America's political system needs to undergo a managed evolution from within—otherwise it simply doesn't matter who is elected president.

ACKNOWLEDGMENTS

Nearly twenty years ago, I was lucky enough to secure a sought-after spot in Professor Joshua Mitchell's seminar on Tocqueville at Georgetown. Though I've generally focused much more on international relations than political theory, Tocqueville's role as an outsider looking in at political systems has continuously inspired me throughout my travels. Having spent about half my life within and half outside the US, it felt like the right time take stock of the many varieties of governance I have encountered over the past two decades.

I am grateful to a select few individuals with whom I shared the entire manuscript, and who graciously provided thoroughly insightful feedback that I've sought to integrate into the final text. Scott Malcomson, my longtime friend, colleague and former editor at the *New York Times*, was once again a source of mature insight on issues ranging from security to technology. Daniel Bell, whose fascinating and evolving work on meritocracy I've been citing for over a decade, continues to inspire with his original approaches to good governance. Peter Ho, Singapore's strategy guru, is both a warm-hearted sage and a living encyclopedia of the crucial decision-making processes through the country's history. My father Sushil has now brandished his pen across five manuscripts and never let me down in attaching a sense of urgency to the problems and solutions I propose. And last but not least, my right-hand researcher Soren Nieminen once again dug up the most interesting historical evidence and scholarly material, no matter how arcane, to further the cause. I'm grateful for all their support and wisdom.

ABOUT THE AUTHOR

Parag Khanna is a Senior Fellow at the Lee Kuan Yew School of Public Policy at the National University of Singapore. He is the author of *Connectography: Mapping the Future of Global Civilization* (2016), *How to Run the World: Charting a Course to the Next Renaissance* (2011) and *The Second World: Empires and Influence in the New Global Order* (2008), as well as co-author of *Hybrid Reality: Thriving in the Emerging Human-Technology Civilization* (2012). In 2008, Parag was named one of Esquire's "75 Most Influential People of the 21st Century," and featured in WIRED magazine's "Smart List." Parag has been a fellow at the Brookings Institution and New Americ Foundation, an adviser to the US National Intelligence Council's *Global Trends 2030 program*, and a senior geopolitical advisor to US Special Operations Forces in Iraq and Afghanistan. He is a Young Global Leader of the World Economic Forum, Councilor of the American Geographical Society, and serves on the board of trustees of the New Cities Foundation. Dr. Khanna holds a PhD in international relations from the London School of Economics, and Bachelor's and Master's degrees from the School of Foreign Service at Georgetown University.

Made in the USA
Middletown, DE
16 August 2017